Published in 2012 by:
Mentor Books Ltd.,
43 Furze Road
Sandyford Industrial Estate
Dublin 18
Republic of Ireland

Tel: +353 1 295 2112/2
Fax: +353 1 295 2114
e-mail: admin@mentorbooks.ie
www.mentorbooks.ie

A catalogue record for this book is available from the British Library
Copyright © Sylvie Cadiou 2012
The right of Sylvie Cadiou to be identified as the author of this work has been asserted by her in accordance with the Copyright, Design and Patents Act 1988.

All rights reserved. No parts of this publication may be reproduced, stored in a retrieval system, or transmitted in any form or by any means electronic, mechanical, photocopying, recording, or otherwise, without prior written permission of the publisher.

ISBN: 978-1-909417-02-1

Editor: Treasa O'Mahony
Cover, typesetting and design: Mary Byrne

Printed in Ireland by Colorman Ltd.

CONTENTS

Introduction: 3

Part 1: Basic Elements 4

Première Partie: Éléments de base.. 4

    Chapter 1: Articles 4

    Chapter 2: Nouns 7

    Chapter 3: Adjectives 9

    Chapter 4: Prepositions and Conjunctions 15

    Chapter 5: Pronouns 20

    Chapter 6: Verbs 27

    Chapter 7: Adverbs 48

Part 2: Going Further.. 50

Deuxième Partie: Approfondissement 50

    Chapter 8: More Tenses 50

    Chapter 9: More Pronouns 58

Part 3: The Sentence.. 66

Troisième Partie: La Phrase 66

    Chapter 10: Putting the Jigsaw Together 66

Grammar Terms in French 75

INTRODUCTION

Grammar is not anything to be scared of. Think of it as a jigsaw puzzle - each piece of a sentence has its place in the language. Together, they all make a beautiful picture!

First, we will have a look in English at some terms used in grammar. This will help you find your way around any other grammar books you may have. The French names for all these grammar terms appear at the end of this book.

It is a good idea to learn these grammar terms in French and English, not only because it makes it easier to navigate a grammar book, but also because it will help you to answer any grammar question in French that you might get in an exam. That's an easy few marks if you know your grammar terms!

Grammar Terms

1. **Articles:** The little words that go before **nouns**.
   There are three main types of articles:
   (a) **Definite articles,** such as *the*.
   (b) **Indefinite articles,** such as *a*.
   (c) **Partitive articles,** such as *some*.

2. **Nouns:** Words that name people, animals, things, places and ideas/concepts.
   In French, nouns are either **masculine** or **feminine** (this is called gender) and they are either in the **singular** or the **plural** (this is called **number**). Names of people, towns, countries etc are called **proper nouns**.

3. **Adjectives:** Words that give more information about a noun; describing words.
   Adjectives are words like *blue* or *tall*. In French, they change according to the gender and number of the noun. This is called agreement; adjectives have to agree with the noun they are describing. You also need to be careful about where they go in a sentence: some go before the noun but most go after the noun. Other types of adjectives are demonstratives, which are words like *this* and *those*, and possessives, which are words like *my* and *your*.

4. **Prepositions and conjunctions:** Those little linking words like *at* and *and*.

5. **Pronouns:** Words that replace nouns to avoid repetition.
   You need to know the **subject pronouns** (he, they etc) and **direct** or **indirect object pronouns** (me, to her, them etc).
   You will also discover reflexive pronouns, as in *s'appeler*, and **disjunctive/stressed** pronouns used after words, such as *chez*.
   Finally, you will need to learn about relative **pronouns**, especially *who* and *whom*.

Complete French Grammar: Part 1

6. **Verbs:** Words used to describe actions or state things.
   When they are untouched, straight out of the dictionary, they are in the **infinitive**. Most verbs follow rules and are therefore called **regular**, but other verbs do not follow any rules and are called **irregular**. In French verbs belong to one of three families, named after the final two letters of their infinitive. You will notice a lot of **ER verbs**, some **IR verbs** and a few **RE verbs**.
   You put verbs in various **tenses** to say when things happened or will happen.
   The basic tenses you need are the **present tense** (actions taking place now or regularly), the **perfect tense** or **passé composé** (what happened), the **future tense** (what will happen) or its very useful alternative the **immediate future** (what is going to happen), and to a lesser extent, the **imperfect** (what was happening, how things were or what used to happen), the **conditional** (what would happen) and the **imperative** (giving advice or making requests).

7. **Adverbs:** Words used to give more information about a verb. In English, they usually end in *–ly* (e.g. *slowly*). The French equivalent of *-ly* is *–ment* (e.g. lentement). Good news! They don't need to agree with anything so you never change their spelling; they are **invariable**.

Part 1: Basic Elements
Première Partie: Éléments de Base

Chapter 1: ARTICLES

In French nouns are rarely used on their own; they need articles. One notable exception to this is when you say what people do for a living, i.e. you don't say *my father is a doctor*; instead you say *my father is doctor* = mon père est docteur. However, if you're talking about **a** or **the doctor**, you would say **un** or **le docteur**.

(a) Definite articles
le - for masculine singular nouns, e.g. le chien = the dog
la - for feminine singular nouns, e.g. la maison = the house
l' - for masculine and feminine singular nouns beginning with a vowel and many nouns beginning with the letter *h*, where that *h* is silent (or *mute*), e.g. l'orange (feminine) = the orange; l'hôpital (masculine) = the hospital
les - for masculine and feminine plural nouns, e.g. les enfants = the children

As you can see, you use these articles when you want to say *the*, i.e. when you want to refer to something specific. You also use definite articles when you want to say you like or don't like something, e.g. j'aime le saumon et la truite mais je n'aime pas les fruits de mer = I like salmon and trout but I don't like seafood.

Chapter 1: Articles

Definite articles are also used to name your subjects in school, e.g. le français, la musique, les maths.
When you are thinking lofty thoughts, you will need to use a definite article with abstract concepts such as la vie (life), la politique (politics) etc.

Definite articles are also used in French with the names of continents and most countries, French regions and provinces, French counties and some towns, e.g. l'Europe, la France, l'Irlande, le Portugal, les Etats-Unis, la Bretagne, le Var, les Landes, Le Havre, La Rochelle.

(b) Indefinite articles

un - for masculine singular nouns, e.g. un cahier = a copy
une - for feminine singular nouns, e.g. une règle = a ruler
des - for masculine and feminine plural nouns, e.g. des crayons = (some) pencils

You use indefinite articles when what you're talking about is not specific. There is a difference between *the dog* and *a dog*, isn't there?
Note the fact that you must use the word des in French, even though there is no need for an article in English.

(c) Partitive articles

du - for masculine singular nouns, e.g. du chocolat = some chocolate
de la - for feminine singular nouns, e.g. de la confiture = some jam
de l' - for masculine and feminine singular nouns beginning with a vowel or a silent *h*, e.g.
de l'huile = some oil; de l'eau = some water
des - for masculine and feminine nouns in the plural, e.g. des petits pois = some peas

These articles must be used in French even though they may not be needed in English. The idea about partitive articles is that you are unlikely to want <u>all</u> the peas in the world but you might like <u>some</u>, a <u>part</u> of the whole.

Note that you can say un/une instead of du/de la/de l' if it makes more sense to say a/one rather then some, e.g. je voudrais un café = I'd like a coffee. In this case, un is similar to one.

On that topic, be careful in French with the expression I'd like an orange meaning I'd like an orange drink. If you say je voudrais une orange, what you're saying is that you'd like the fruit, not the drink. Try using a brand name instead. Here's a French orange drink to try: je voudrais un Orangina.

There is one more thing to be careful with: in English, you say I have a brother but I don't have *any* sisters. In French, that sentence is J'ai un frère mais je n'ai pas *de* sœurs.
The French equivalent of the word **any** in a negative sentence is **de** or **d'**.

5

Complete French Grammar: Part 1

EXERCICES

1. Read the following sentences and **choose the correct article** from the three options provided. Make sure you are able to **explain** your choice.
(a) Je déteste **un/le/du** poulet.
_____

(b) Il mange **du/de l'/de la** pain avec **la/de la/des** confiture.
_____

(c) On a acheté **une/la/un** nouvelle voiture.
_____

(d) Chez moi, en haut, il y a **un/une/les** chambre et **un/les/des** toilettes.
_____

(e) Je n'ai pas **de l'/des/d'** argent pour acheter **un/une/du** livre.
_____

2. Read the following sentences and **decide whether an article is needed in the gap or not.** Then, **fill such gaps** with a suitable choice.
(a) _____ Paris est _____ capitale de _____ France.
(b) J'ai _____ frère et _____ sœur.
(c) Je voudrais _____ frites, j'adore _____ frites!
(d) _____ parents de Vlad sont polonais.
(e) Ma tante est _____ infirmière.

3. Translate the following sentences into French:
(a) I love sport, soccer, rugby, hockey...
_____

(b) He has a school bag, books and copies.
_____

(c) In school, she studies French and German.
_____

(d) I would like a sandwich with some tea.
_____

(e) The plates are in a press in the kitchen.
_____

Chapter 2: NOUNS

The Gender Issue

I'm sure you've often bemoaned the fact that French nouns have a masculine or a feminine form. You can blame the Latin language for that! There are unfortunately no signs of the Académie Française, the organisation in charge of the French language, getting rid of gender in French nouns any day soon.

The best way to cope with this problem is to learn any new noun with its article, i.e. don't just learn maison, learn une maison or la maison. Here are some useful tips on French nouns:
- Most nouns have only one gender, which can seem strange sometimes. Une souris is a mouse, no matter whether we're talking about a male or a female mouse.
- Some nouns can have two genders without any change to their spelling, e.g. un artiste, une artiste.
- Other nouns will change slightly from masculine to feminine, e.g. un boulanger, une boulangère. In this example, the masculine -er became -ère in the feminine. In the same way, you would usually change -eur to –euse (vendeur/vendeuse), -teur to -teuse (chanteur/chanteuse) or sometimes to –trice (agriculteur/agricultrice), -ien to -ienne (pharmacien/pharmacienne).
- Gender can be vital for the meaning of a word, e.g. le livre = the book but la livre = the pound, so they do not mean quite the same thing!

So, is there an easier way to correctly guess the gender of nouns? Well, most words used to describe people are masculine for boys/men and feminine for girls/women, e.g. mon frère et ma sœur. This also applies if you're referring to male or female animals, e.g. un chat/une chatte.

Here are some more clues:
- Nouns ending in –ment are usually masculine, e.g. le gouvernement.
- Nouns ending in –age/-ail/-al/-as/-eu/-eux/-oir/-ou also tend to be masculine.
- Other masculine nouns include: chemical substances, gases and metals (le carbone, le fer), colours (le bleu), dates, seasons, months, days of the week (le 14 juillet, le printemps, le lundi) and languages (le français).
- Nouns ending in –tion are usually feminine, e.g. la natation.
- Nouns ending in –ance/-anse/-ence/-ense/-ée/-elle/-esse/-ette/-otte/-euse/-ière/-ienne /-onne/-rie/-sie/-sion/-tie/-ture also tend to be feminine.
- Other feminine nouns include a lot of words ending in e, such as countries (la Grèce),
- flowers (la tulipe), fruit and vegetables (la fraise, la carotte), clothes (la chemise),
- illnesses (la grippe), rivers (la Loire), sciences (la chimie) and leisure activities (la peinture).

But remember, there are *always* exceptions …

Complete French Grammar: Part 1

The Plural Form

To put a noun into the plural in French, you usually just add an s, as you do in English. But just as the English language has some exceptions (e.g. *child/children*), so it is with the French language, only more so of course! Here is a short list of irregular plurals:

- Nouns ending in s, x, z in the singular don't change in the plural, e.g. le nez, les nez.
- Most nouns ending in au, eau, eu in the singular take an x, not an s in the plural, e.g. un bateau, deux bateaux.
- Most nouns ending in -al in the singular will end in -aux in the plural, e.g. un animal, des animaux. Notable exceptions to this rule are bal, festival and carnaval, which take an s in the plural.
- Just seven nouns ending in –ou in the singular will end in –oux in the plural. They are: bijou (jewel), caillou (rock/stone), chou (cabbage), genou (knee), hibou (owl), joujou (baby speak for toy), pou (louse). All the others end in s in the plural.
- Some nouns change totally from the singular to the plural, but luckily they are very few. You know les yeux, but did you know that one eye = un œil?
- Proper nouns tend not to change, unless you are talking about royal families. Hence the ordinary les Dupont but the royal les Tudors.
- Some nouns will only be used in the plural, such as les mathématiques.
- Some nouns change pronunciation in the plural, such as un œuf (pronounced 'uff'), des œufs (pronounced 'uh').

EXERCICES

1. Masculine or feminine? Using your notes, **decide the gender** of the following nouns:

bouchère _____   rose (the colour) _____
travail   _____   jeu _____
asperge   _____   pollution _____
danse   _____   Portugal _____
rose (the flower) _____   parlement _____

2. Translate the following sentences into French:

(a) My sister is a baker but also a singer.
_____

(b) I have sore knees, I fell on the rocks.
_____

(c) I have blue eyes but my friend has one green eye and one blue eye.
_____

(d) There were two festivals about animals.
_____

(e) I love red and silver.
_____

Chapter 3: ADJECTIVES

Adjectives are **describing** words used to give more information about the noun.
When using adjectives, remember to make them **agree** with the noun they are describing and make sure you know whether they go **before** or **after** the noun.

The Gender and Number of Adjectives

In French, the usual way of making an adjective feminine is to add an e to the masculine form (e.g. il est grand/elle est grande), unless it already ends in e, in which case, you do nothing (e.g. il est belge/elle est belge)!

To make an adjective plural, all you usually do is add an s to the masculine or feminine singular form (e.g. ils sont grands/elles sont grandes). If the masculine singular form already ends in an s or an x, don't add another one in the masculine plural; one is plenty!

But, let's face it, this is French, so where would we be without (quite) a few exceptions!

- First, we'll deal with adjectives that **don't change at all** in the feminine or the plural. These types of adjectives usually come from nouns and relate to colour, e.g. marron (brown), châtain (light brown, for hair), orange, noisette (hazel), olive, bronze, argent (silver) and or (gold).
  When two ordinary adjectives of colour join forces, e.g. bleu clair (light blue) or rouge foncé (dark red), they too always stay the same. Compare: une robe bleue but une robe bleu clair.
- With most masculine singular adjectives ending in –eil/-el/-et/-ien/-ol/-on, double that last consonant to form the feminine and add -e/-es as usual, e.g. ancien (masculine singular)/ancienne (feminine singular)/anciennes (feminine plural).
- Other adjectives follow that double consonant pattern, e.g. bas/basse = low; gentil/gentille = kind; gros/grosse = fat; gras/grasse = fatty/greasy; épais/épaisse = thick; moyen/moyenne = average.
- Note that some adjectives ending in -et will end with -ète in the feminine instead of doubling the final consonant, e.g. complet/complète = complete; inquiet/inquiète = worried; discret/discrète = discreet; secret/secrète = secret.
- This pattern also applies to most adjectives ending in –er in the masculine singular. Their feminine singular form will end in –ère, e.g. cher/chère.
- Most adjectives ending in –eux or –ieux in the masculine singular will end in –euse or -ieuse in the feminine singular, e.g. heureux/heureuse = happy; curieux/curieuse = curious/nosy.
- Adjectives ending in –if or -euf in the masculine singular will end in –ive and -euve respectively, e.g. sportif/sportive = sporty; neuf/neuve = brand new.
- As is the case with nouns, most adjectives ending in –eur in the masculine singular end in –euse in the feminine singular. Those ending in –teur end in –teuse or sometimes –trice, e.g. prometteur/prometteuse = promising.

- And of course there are adjectives for which these small changes are not enough! In their case, the feminine singular form is quite different from the masculine singular. Here are the usual suspects:
blanc(s)/blanche(s) = white - linked to the verb 'to blanch'
doux/douce(s) = soft or gentle - linked to the word 'dulcet' as in 'dulcet tones'
favori(s)/favorite(s) = favourite
faux/fausse(s) = false
frais/fraîche(s) = fresh
long(s)/longue(s) = long
public(s)/publique(s) = public
sec(s)/sèche(s) = dry
roux/rousse(s) = red-haired or reddish - linked to the word 'russet'

You may have noticed that a lot of the words above resemble English. That's no accident. Words get borrowed all the time between languages. It seems that the feminine singular of French adjectives was chosen over the masculine when the borrowing happened. Try saying the feminine form of the adjectives above out loud and you'll be convinced!

- Other adjectives are not happy with just changing their feminine singular forms, they want more! The adjectives below have an extra form to be used in the masculine singular when the noun that follows the adjective starts with a vowel or a silent **h**. beau(x)/**bel**/belle(s) = beautiful, e.g. un beau sac/un **bel** oiseau; nouveau(x) **nouvel** nouvelle(s) = new, e.g. un nouveau pull/le **Nouvel;** An vieux/**vieil**/vieille(s) = old, e.g. un vieux château/un **vieil** homme
- Finally, a word about the term new. You have a choice of two words in French, depending on which 'new' you mean: new in general terms and also new to *you* = nouveau; brand new is neuf, e.g. une nouvelle voiture is a newly acquired car, but not necessarily fresh from the showroom, whereas une voiture neuve is brand new and shiny!

Position of Adjectives

Most adjectives in French appear after the noun, contrary to English. Colours, for example, hardly ever come before the noun.
However, a few adjectives appear **before** their noun. As some of them are very common, it's a good idea to learn them by heart.

Here's a selection of those adjectives which defy the general rule and go before their noun:

beau(x)/bel/belle(s) = beautiful
joli(s)/jolie(s) = pretty
jeune(s) = young
vieux/vieil/vieille(s) = old
nouveau(x)/nouvel/nouvelle(s) = new

bon(s)/bonne(s) = good
mauvais/mauvaise(s) = bad
gentil(s)/gentille(s) = kind
grand(s)/grande(s) = tall*
petit(s)/petite(s) = small

gros/grosse(s) = fat
haut(s)/haute(s) = high -
except in some set expressions such as des talons hauts = high heels
long(s)/longue(s) = long - except in some set expressions such as les cheveux longs = long hair
premier(s)/première(s) = first, second(s)/seconde(s) = second,
deuxième(s) = second, troisième(s) = third etc

*When describing people, grand can cause a few problems. If you see the expression un grand homme, it usually means an important, respected man so it is better to say un homme grand if you mean a tall man. It could be said that Général De Gaulle, who was both very tall and an important politician, was un grand homme grand!

Some adjectives **change meaning** depending on whether you use them before or after the noun. Here are some of them:

ancien = former/ancient, e.g. un ancien élève = a former pupil; un château ancien = an ancient castle

dernier = last/the last, e.g. dimanche dernier = last Sunday; le dernier dimanche = the last Sunday

pauvre = poor, e.g. une pauvre femme = a wretched woman; une femme pauvre = a penniless woman

propre = clean/own, e.g. une chambre propre = a clean bedroom; ma propre chambre = my own bedroom

Comparatives and Superlatives

In other words, how to express more/as/less ... than, and the most ... /the least... .

- more ... than = **plus ... que,** e.g. il est plus grand que son frère = he is taller than his brother
- as ... as = **aussi ... que**, e.g. elle est aussi gentille que sa sœur = she is as nice as her sister
- less ... than = **moins ... que**, e.g. nous sommes moins fatigués qu'hier = we're less tired than yesterday
- the most ... = **le plus ... / la plus ... / les plus**, e.g. Je suis la plus jeune et Marc est le plus petit, mais on est les plus rapides! = I'm the youngest and Marc is the smallest but we're the fastest!
- the least ... = **le moins ... / la moins ... / les moins ...**, e.g. J'ai acheté le jean le moins cher, la chemise la moins chère et les chaussures les moins chères! = I bought the cheapest pair of jeans, the cheapest shirt and the cheapest shoes!

Note the agreement of the adjectives in these sentences.

Complete French Grammar: Part 1

There are of course a couple of adjectives that do things differently, such as these two:
- **bon** (good) becomes **meilleur** for better and **le/la/les meilleur(e)(s)** for the best.
- **mauvais** (bad) becomes **pire** for worse and **le/la/les pire(s)** for the worst, although you can usually get away with saying **plus mauvais** for worse and **le/la/les plus mauvais(e)(es)** for the worst.

The adjectives we have seen so far are those that most people would use as examples if they were asked **What is an adjective?** However, there are other words that also belong to the adjective family as you will learn in the next section.

Demonstrative Adjectives

They are the words for this, that, these, those, and that's it! So, not a long list here:

ce – used with a masculine singular noun, e.g. ce livre = this book
cet – used with masculine singular nouns starting with a vowel or a silent h, e.g. cet ordinateur = this computer; cet homme = this man
cette – used with a feminine singular noun, e.g. cette fille = this girl
ces – used with a masculine or feminine noun in the plural, e.g. ces filles et ces garçons = these girls and these boys

Strangely, the word for afternoon can be used either in the masculine or the feminine, so you will come across cet après-midi and cette après-midi for this afternoon. They are both correct.

In English, there is a slight difference in meaning between this and that, and between these and those. The French words don't make that distinction. You will need to add something after the noun to do that.
this book = ce livre-**ci**
that book = ce livre-**là**
these pens = ces stylos-**ci**
those pens = ces stylos-**là**

The word ci is short for ici, which means here. Remember the word voici? It comes from vois ici, meaning see here. The word là is one of the words for there, also present in the word voilà.

Possessive Adjectives

They are the words for my, your, his etc. In French a possessive adjective can be made up of 3 words – this is because they must agree with the noun that follows them. That's an important consideration, especially when it comes to saying his and her. In English, you use his when the 'owner' is male and her when the 'owner' is female. This rule never applies in French, as the possessive adjectives agree with 'what is owned', not with the 'owner'.

Chapter 3: Adjectives

For example, when somebody says her sister in English, we know that we are talking about two females, whereas in French, when you say sa sœur, it could mean her sister but it could also mean his sister and possibly its sister! All sa is doing is agreeing with sœur, which is a feminine singular noun. Is your head still ok?!

	For masculine singular nouns	For any singular nouns starting with vowel or a silent **h**	For feminine singular nouns	For masculine and feminine a plural nouns
MY	mon	mon	ma	mes
YOUR (casual)	ton	ton	ta	tes
HIS / HER / ITS	son	son	sa	ses
OUR	notre	notre	notre	nos
YOUR (polite or group)	votre	votre	votre	vos
THEIR	leur	leur	leur	leurs

Here are some examples of possessive adjectives in action:

Mon amie Charlotte et **son** frère Alex sont allés chez **leurs** cousins l'été dernier.
Note the use of mon with amie even though we're talking about a girl. That's because amie starts with a vowel. Similarly, son is used because frère is masculine, even though Charlotte is a girl. We must use leurs for their since cousins is in the plural.

One last word: please use the correct possessive adjective with family members! You know what gender they are! No examiner wants to read about mon mère and ma père.

EXERCICES

1. Choose the correct form of the adjective from the three options given. Then, **re-write** the sentence, putting the adjective in the **correct place. Explain** your answers.

(a) J'ai un chien (noir/noire/noirs)
_____
(b) On a acheté un gâteau (bon/bonne/bonnes)
_____
(c) Regarde la maison! (grand/grande/grands) + (blanc/blance/blanche)
_____
(d) C'est une usine (ancien/anciene/ancienne)
_____
(e) C'est un ours (=bear) (beau/bel/belle) + (brun/brune/bruns)
_____

13

Complete French Grammar: Part 1

EXERCICES

2. Fill in the gaps with the required adjective. Be careful with gender and number.
   (a) Mon grand-père est (old) _____ mais c'est encore un (handsome) _____ homme.
   (b) J'ai eu des (good) _____ notes en histoire.
   (c) Je vais mettre mes chaussures (black) _____ ou (brown) _____ et ma chemise (light blue) _____ .
   (d) Marie est (happy) _____, elle a eu (the best) _____ résultat en maths.

3. Fill in the gaps with the required **demonstrative** adjective or **possessive** adjective.
   (a) À quelle heure est-ce que tu as pris (your) _____ car (this) _____ matin?
   (b) (My) _____ correspondante s'appelle Arielle. (Her) _____ père est pharmacien.
   (c) Ils vont passer (their) _____ vacances dans (this) _____ hôtel.
   (d) (This) _____ maison est plus jolie que (our) _____ appartement.
   (e) (Their) _____ chat est beau, il est blanc, (his) _____ yeux sont verts et (his) _____ queue est noire.

Chapter 4: PREPOSITIONS AND CONJUNCTIONS

These are the words used to link sentences – and parts of sentences – together. You use them all the time in English. Here's a simple sentence in French with quite a few of them in it:
Yvan et Marianne vont **au** cinéma **avec** Patrick **à** huit heures.

We'll look at **prepositions** from English to French first, as it's usually when translating your ideas from English to French that problems occur.

- **in**

dans, e.g. dans mon jardin
en, e.g. en 2050

- **in/to**

à, e.g. à Paris
en, e.g. en Irlande, en ville (It is also used with languages, e.g. en anglais)

Remember that when you say, for example, to do, the to is part of the infinitive and therefore does not translate in French: to do = faire

- **at**

à, e.g. à dix heures, à Noël

- **in/to/at somebody's house or place of business**

chez, e.g. chez ma tante, chez le docteur
To say at home, you can use à la maison or chez moi/chez nous

- **at the/in the/to the**

dans = inside

You can use dans for in if there's a feeling of 'boundaries' to your expression, e.g. dans le comté de Wexford (counties have borders), dans la chambre (rooms have walls) etc. Otherwise, you will need to use *à* plus the articles *le, la, l'* and *les*. Remember what happens, though:

> à + le = **au**
> à + la = **à la**
> à + l' = **à l'**
> à + les = **aux**

Complete French Grammar: Part 1

You use **au** with masculine countries, e.g. je vais **au** Portugal (I'm going **to** Portugal), elle habite **au** Danemark (she lives **in** Denmark).

Aux is used with plural countries, e.g. je vais **aux** Etats-Unis (I'm going **to the** United States)

You will also need these prepositions with the verb jouer when you talk about games, e.g. je joue au foot and in the expression of pain j'ai mal à… , e.g. j'ai mal **aux** dents.

Remember that to say at the weekend you do not use any preposition, you have to say **le** weekend.

- **on**

En route/en chemin = on the way

To say on one's own, you can use tout(e) seul(e)

When on is part of the verb in English, there is usually no preposition in the French equivalent, e.g. s'entendre = to get on; mettre = to put on

- **from**

de/d', e.g. il vient de Rome (he comes from Rome), une carte d'Edith (a card from Edith)
de la part de = on behalf of

- **from the**

You use de plus the articles le, la, l' and les. Again, remember what happens:

> de + le = **du**
> de + la = **de la**
> de + l' = **de l'**
> de + les = **des**

With feminine countries, you can choose whether to say de or de la, e.g. elle vient de Belgique or elle vient *de la* Belgique.

You will also use this list with the verb jouer when you talk about instruments and also with the verb faire when discussing leisure activities, e.g. je joue du piano, je fais de l'athlétisme.

Chapter 4: Prepositions and Conjunctions

- **of/'s**

de/d', e.g. beaucoup de monde (a lot of people), l'anniversaire d' Aurélie (Aurélie's birthday)
de is also used in a few phrases with avoir, such as:
avoir peur de = to be afraid of
avoir besoin de = to need
avoir envie de = to feel like/to want
When you follow these expressions with a verb, the *-ing* at the end of that verb in English will be an infinitive in French, e.g. je n'ai pas envie de travailler (I don't feel like working).

In the French expressions for too much or enough, de is also used with a noun, e.g. j'ai trop de devoirs (I've got too much homework), tu as assez d'argent? (do you have enough money?)

- **made of**

en
Examples:
une table en bois = a wooden table
un bracelet en or = a gold bracelet
une veste en cuir = a leather jacket
un pull en laine = a woolly jumper

- **for**

(a) pour
Examples:
un cadeau pour ma copine = a present for my friend
ils partent pour une semaine = they're going for a week
(b) depuis
Example:
je le connais depuis six ans = I've known him for six years
Note that depuis is also used to express since.
Example:
Je le connais depuis l'école primaire = I've known him since Primary school
To say for a long time, say depuis longtemps.
The word for during is pendant. It is a better choice than pour in expressions such as for my holidays.

- **around**

(a) autour de, e.g. il y a une rocade autour de la ville = there's a bypass around the town
(b) près de = near, e.g. il y a une poste près d'ici? = is there a post office around here?
(c) vers, e.g. je t'appellerai vers cinq heures = I'll call you at around five
(d) environ, e.g. ça coûte environ vingt euros = it costs around €20

17

Complete French Grammar: Part 1

- **with/without**

avec, e.g. je suis en vacances avec mes parents = I'm on holidays with my parents
sans, e.g. nous sommes partis sans elle = we left without her

- **by**

par, e.g. on est passés par Paris = we went by/through Paris
de, e.g. c'est un livre de Victor Hugo = it's a book by Victor Hugo
en, e.g. ils sont venus en avion = they came by plane
se débrouiller = to get by, to manage

We will now look at the main **conjunctions**. You will soon discover that you already know them well!

but = mais
or = ou
and = et
if = si
as/like = comme
because = parce que

Other useful expressions are:
as soon as = **dès que**, e.g. je te téléphonerai dès que je serai arrivé = I'll call you as soon as I arrive

therefore = donc, e.g. 'je pense donc je suis' = 'I think therefore I am'
(Quote from René Descartes)

as well as = ainsi que (formal), e.g. Madame de Blois invita le Comte ainsi que le Duc = Lady Blois invited the Count as well as the Duke

either ... or = soit ..., soit ..., e.g. tu prends soit le car, soit le train = you take either the coach or the train

neither ... nor = ne + ni ..., ni ..., e.g. je n'aime ni la viande, ni le poisson = I like neither meat nor fish

Chapter 4: Prepositions and Conjunctions

1. Fill in the gaps with the correct preposition. You may have to check the gender of the nouns used in the exercise first. **Explain** your answers.
(a) On va _____ piscine et _____ cinéma demain.
(b) Il est arrivé _____ Cork _____ onze heures.
(c) Je joue _____ violon, je joue _____ hockey et je fais _____ équitation.
(d) _____ weekend, je fais la grasse matinée et l'après-midi, je vais _____ ville.
(e) On sera _____ Espagne _____ 10 _____ 30 juillet.

2. Fill in the gaps with a suitable conjunction. **Explain** your answers.
(a) Je prends mon café _____ sucre. En fait, je ne prends _____ sucre, _____ lait.
(b) _____ les vacances, j'ai visité Londres _____ ma famille.
(c) Il est beau _____ stupide!
(d) _____ j'avais le temps, j'ai fait du lèche-vitrine.
(e) Je n'aime pas la chimie _____ c'est difficile.
(f) _____ tu veux, on peut aller au Café des Sports _____ au Café de Paris.

3. Translate the following text into French:
On Wednesday, I went to my grandfather's house with my sister Mina. We played cards. On Friday, at around four o' clock I went to the supermarket for my mum. At the weekend, I helped with the chores in the house. On Saturday night, as there was nothing on TV, I listened to some music in my bedroom.

Chapter 5: PRONOUNS

Subject pronouns

Let's start with a quick look again at the **subject pronouns**.

The job of **pronouns** is to replace nouns in order to avoid repetition in a story. For example, imagine you are describing your best friend (mon meilleur ami). Here's how you could start:

Mon meilleur ami s'appelle Tom, mon meilleur ami a quinze ans, mon meilleur ami est grand et brun, mon meilleur ami aime le hurling etc.

All this is correct French but do you see what's happening? You're getting a cramp writing mon meilleur ami so many times and your work sounds like a child's story. Pronouns to the rescue! Mon meilleur ami should be replaced by il and your story will become much better!

The pronouns we're looking at here are called **subject** pronouns because they are the grammatical subjects of the verb, in other words, they do the action. Look at the following example: David regarde le film = David is watching the film.
David is **the subject** because he's the one doing the watching.

JE (or J' in front of a vowel or a silent *h*)	I
TU	YOU, one person only, someone that you're friendly with or related to (this is usually referred to as the **casual you** in grammar books)
IL	HE or IT
ELLE	SHE or IT
CE/ÇA (CECI/CELA)	a very abstract IT, as in the phrase Ça va
ON	a casual WE (very useful, as you use it with the he/she form of the verb) or an equivalent to the English one or you/they if used in the abstract.
NOUS	WE, quite formal
VOUS	YOU, one person that you have to be polite to **or** a group of people (Youse or Ye!)
ILS	THEY, an all-masculine group **or** a mixed gender group
ELLES	THEY, an all-feminine group

Let's see a few examples where we will replace the words in italics with a subject pronoun:
la fille joue au tennis → *elle* joue au tennis
le chat est sur la table → *il* est sur la table
ma copine et moi irons au stade → *nous* irons au stade
toi et ton copain irez aussi au stade → *vous* irez aussi au stade
Paul et Sandra sont sympas → *ils* sont sympas

EXERCICES

Identify and then replace the subjects of the following sentences with a suitable **subject pronoun.** Remember that a subject can be a group of words.
(a) Madame Leclerc habite en Auvergne. _____
(b) La table est en bois. _____
(c) Ma famille et moi sommes en Espagne. _____
(d) Le bel oiseau rouge et jaune chante bien. _____
(e) Les touristes sont à la plage. _____

Object pronouns

Object pronouns are the **objects** of the verb, in other words, the action is done to *them*. The term **object** does not refer to the usual meaning of the word as a 'thing'; it's more in the sense of the *objective*, the *target* of the action.
Look at our example again:

David regarde le film

Now, if we look at the words le film, we see that the film is not doing any watching, it is being watched. The action is done to it. The film is the **object** in that sentence.

What happens if you want to replace le film? You might want to add another sentence, where you give more information, such as the fact that David is watching the film in the sitting-room. Again, as with the earlier example of mon meilleur ami, you can replace le film with a pronoun. As le film is the **object**, you'll need an **object pronoun**.

The French language differentiates between **direct** object pronouns and **indirect** object pronouns. No, no, don't run away, it's not that bad!
This has everything to do with the use of that lovely little preposition à. Let's have a look at another example:

Patricia donne la clé à Sébastien = Patricia gives the key to Sébastien

Complete French Grammar: Part 1

The verb donne has two objects: (a) the key that is given and (b) the recipient of the key, Sébastien. But when we look more closely, we see that Sébastien is not alone but is accompanied by à (= to). That's the difference between direct and indirect objects in a nutshell. If you have a to/à in the original sentence, you need an **indirect object pronoun.***

* Watch out for some verbs that have à in French but no to in English, such as to phone = téléphoner à or to ask someone = demander à. In these cases, use the French structure and indirect object pronouns.

Direct and Indirect Object Pronouns

ME	ME (or M')
TO ME	ME (or M')
YOU	TE (or T')
TO YOU	TE (or T')
HIM/IT	LE (or L')
TO HIM/TO IT	LUI
HER/IT	LA (or L')
TO HER/TO IT	LUI
US	NOUS
TO US	NOUS
YOU	VOUS
TO YOU	VOUS
THEM	LES
TO THEM	LEUR

As you can see, it's only with the **third persons** that you'll have to do a bit of mental gymnastics, i.e. **me** and **to me** are the same but **him/her/it** and **to him/to her/to it** as well as **them** and to **them** are different.

Let's see some examples, where we'll replace the nouns with an object pronoun.
le garçon → direct → le
la clé → direct → la
l'orange → direct → la or l' (it will depend on the spelling of the following word)
à ta mère → indirect → lui
à son père → indirect → lui
toi et ta sœur → direct → vous
mes chaussures → direct → les
à mes parents → indirect → leur

Chapter 5: Pronouns

You may wonder why full sentences were not used in the examples.
Well, that's because there's another little problem…
It's to do with **where** the object pronouns go in a sentence. It may look strange but the French put them **before the verb**. This means that I watch it becomes I it watch.
  And there's more: if you're using a verb plus an infinitive, the pronoun(s) goes **before the infinitive** only, so your sentence would now read I am going to it watch.
Simple!

Look at these examples:
Je regarde *le film* → le film, direct object → it = le → je **le** regarde.
Paul parle *à ses amis* → à ses amis, indirect object → to them = leur → Paul **leur** parle.
Je vais regarder *le film* → je vais **le** regarder.
Paul aime parler *à ses amis* → Paul aime **leur** parler

So how do you know which object pronoun comes first when there's two or more of them?
Well: (a) direct object pronouns come before indirect object pronouns
     (b) some direct object pronouns come before others, like this:

me	le	lui
te	la	leur
nous	les	
vous		

So if you wanted to replace all the nouns in our previous example – Patricia donne la clé à Sébastien – you replace Patricia with the subject pronoun elle, you replace la clé with the direct object pronoun la, and you replace à Sébastien with the indirect object pronoun lui. The subject, elle, comes first, of course. Then we have to sort out the order of the object pronouns. Looking at the grid, we see that la comes before lui. Then, we must remember to add the verb.
Ok, here goes: elle la lui donne. Pure poetry!

EXERCICES

Replace the blue words with an **object pronoun** and **rewrite** the sentence putting the pronoun(s) in the **correct place**.
  (a) Je lis le journal. _____
  (b) Je téléphonerai à Marie. _____
  (c) Elle achète les tickets. _____
  (d) J'ai trouvé mon pull. _____
  (e) Ils vont visiter le château. _____
  (f) Pia montre son nouveau portable à sa copine._____
  (g) Je vais parler à mes parents. _____
  (h) J'aimerais donner cette carte à ma prof de français. _____
  _____

Complete French Grammar: Part 1

Reflexive pronouns

One of the first verbs you learnt in French was *s'appeler*. You had to learn to say je **m'**appelle, il **s'**appelle, nous **nous** appelons etc, remembering to put those extra words in.

Those extra words are what we call **reflexive pronouns**, as they reflect back on the person talking. You could translate je *m'*appelle Jack as I call *myself* Jack. Remember, however, that there are verbs that exist both with or without a reflexive pronoun. Example: laver and se laver, e.g. Rémi lave sa voiture (Rémi washes his car) as opposed to Rémi se lave (Rémi washes himself).

Here is the list of **reflexive pronouns**:

For JE, add:	ME or M'
For TU, add:	TE or T'
For IL, add:	SE or S'
For ELLE, add:	SE or S'
For ÇA, add:	SE or S'
For ON, add:	SE or S'
For NOUS, add:	NOUS
For VOUS, add:	VOUS
For ILS, add:	SE or S'
For ELLES, add:	SE or S'

Examples:
je me lave
tu te réveilles
il se douche
elle se dépêche
ça se sent
on s'habille
nous nous couchons
vous vous levez
ils s'entendent bien
elles se disputent

Remember, reflexive verbs are **normal** verbs, they are usually regular and the only thing different about them is the reflexive pronoun so there is no need to avoid them!

Chapter 5: Pronouns

Stressed or disjunctive pronouns

These are pronouns that you use when you want to **emphasise** the subject (that's what the stressed name refers to) or if you're using a pronoun **after a preposition or conjunction**, e.g. Moi, j'aime le chou or Je viendrai chez toi.

These pronouns are also used in the expression myself, yourself etc. (as in I made this myself), where the self bit is même and the my, your etc is one of these pronouns, e.g. I made this myself = je l'ai fait moi-même.

Stressed pronouns:

To emphasise JE, use:	MOI
To emphasise TU, use:	TOI
To emphasise IL, or another masculine singular noun, use:	LUI
To emphasise ELLE, or another feminine singular noun, use:	ELLE
To emphasise NOUS, or ON when meaning we, use:	NOUS
To emphasise VOUS, use:	VOUS
To emphasise ILS or another masculine or mixed plural, use:	EUX
To emphasise ELLES or another feminine plural, use :	ELLES

EXERCICES

Fill in the gaps with the correct stressed pronoun:
(a) Ils sont rentrés chez _____ à dix heures et _____, on est rentrés chez _____ à minuit.
(b) Ça, c'est pour Nadine, pour _____ toute seule, ok ?
(c) _____, il est super-intelligent !
(d) J'ai appris à nager _____ - même.

Complete French Grammar: Part 1

Relative pronouns

We now come to a very important type of pronoun called **relative pronouns**. You might know them already. We will look at two of the most useful ones:

qui/que

Have you ever written something like, j'ai un frère qui a douze ans? If so, you used a relative pronoun. That pronoun is qui and it translates as who: I have a brother who is 12.

You can see that qui allows you to add information about the brother. Did you notice that this information contains a verb: is? However this particular verb is not the main verb. That's the key point, here. You need a word linking a noun (in this case, brother) to any **secondary** verb (in this case, is) and that word is a relative pronoun.

Now look at this example: I have a brother whom I love.
In English you use who in who is 12 but whom in whom I love.
Whats the difference?
Look at the two constructions closely: **(a)** I have a brother who is 12.
(b) I have a brother whom I love.

(a) who is 12: the **verb** = is and its **subject** = who, referring to brother.

(b) whom I love: the **verb** = love and its **subject** = I, <u>not</u> the brother. The brother is the **object** of the love. Whom is therefore the **object**, since it refers to the brother.

You do the same in French: **qui** is the relative pronoun for the **subject**
que is the relative pronoun for the **object**.

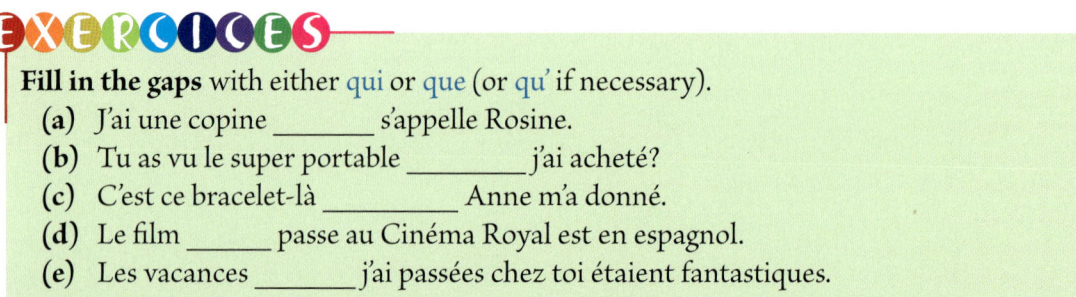

J'ai un frère qui a 12 ans   J'ai un frère que j'adore

Note that que becomes qu' in front of a vowel or a silent/mute **h**. Qui never changes.

EXERCICES

Fill in the gaps with either qui or que (or qu' if necessary).
  (a) J'ai une copine _____ s'appelle Rosine.
  (b) Tu as vu le super portable _____ j'ai acheté?
  (c) C'est ce bracelet-là _____ Anne m'a donné.
  (d) Le film _____ passe au Cinéma Royal est en espagnol.
  (e) Les vacances _____ j'ai passées chez toi étaient fantastiques.

Chapter 6: VERBS

When you look up a verb in the dictionary, it is given to you in the **infinitive**, meaning the most basic form of the verb before anything is done to it. In English, infinitives are the **to** form of the verb, e.g. to play.

The infinitive in French can be used in a sentence but it will nearly always be with another verb, e.g. je vais jouer = I am going to play.

It is also used to express the *–ing* form of an English verb, when that *–ing* form has the meaning of to, e.g. I like playing (= to play) football = j'aime *jouer* au football.

All infinitives in French end in ER, IR or RE. This is an obvious way of grouping them, which is why you have three families of verbs: the **ER verbs**, the **IR verbs** and the **RE verbs.** Of these three families, the ER verb family is by far the biggest. The majority of ER verbs are **regular verbs.**

Regular verbs, from the word règle meaning rule, are well-behaved verbs that follow the same rules. Once you learn a rule, all regular verbs will follow it, enabling you to use verbs you may not have known before.
But of course, in every good family, there is a black sheep or two. French verb families have their black sheep too; they are called **irregular verbs**. In other words, they do not follow rules. With them, all bets are off. You therefore have to **learn** how they behave in the present tense, the passé composé etc on a case by case basis.

The most useful irregular verbs to know are:
- **avoir** = **to have**
- **être** = **to be**
- **aller** = **to go**
- **faire** = **to do or to make**
- **prendre** = **to take**

You can call these the *Famous Five* (*Le Club Des Cinq* in French!).

Tenses

A verb will change according to the **subject** used but also according to the **tense** you're using, i.e. a verb in the future (je jouerai = I will play) does not look like a verb in the past (je jouais - I used to play) - how else would we know which is which?!

Complete French Grammar: Part 1

A quick overview of essential tenses
Example: **jouer** with *je* as the subject:

Gone By	Now or Regularly	Yet to Come	Unsure
Passé Composé -What happened e.g. j'ai joué	**Present tense** -What happens -What is happening e.g. je joue	**Present with context** e.g. je joue demain **Future** -What will happen e.g. je jouerai	**Conditional** -What would happen e.g. je jouerais
Imperfect -How it was -What was happening -What used to happen e.g. je jouais			
Immediate Past -What just happened e.g. je viens de jouer		**Immediate Future** -What is going to happen e.g. je vais jouer	

The Present Tense

You use the **present tense** to say **how things are**, e.g. I am tall; she is Irish.
You also use the **present tense** to say **what you do regularly** and **what you're doing right now**.
In English, there are two different way of spelling your verb. In French, there is only one:

> *I do* French in school = je *fais* du français à l'école
> *I'm doing* French at the moment = je *fais* du français en ce moment

You have to say *do*.
This applies to all verbs, not just *faire*, e.g. she sings or she is singing = elle chante.

The **present tense** is also used in phrases with depuis (since/for).
Example: il travaille ici depuis six mois.
That sentence in English would be he *has been working* here for six months.

Formation of the Present Tense with Regular Verbs
As regular verbs follow rules, your task can be simplified by learning the rules for each tense. You don't have to learn each verb individually, like you have to do with irregular verbs. Here is the rule for putting a regular verb in the **present tense**:

> 1. Remove the ER, IR or RE from the infinitive. This gives you the stem. You will have to add endings to the stem.
> 2. Add the correct **ending** to the stem, according to the grid on the top of the next page:

Chapter 6: Verbs

	For **ER** verbs, add:	For **IR** verbs, add:	For **RE** verbs, add:
For **je**	e	is	s
For **tu**	es	is	s
For **il; elle; ce; ça; on**	e	it	(nothing)
For **nous**	ons	issons	ons
For **vous**	ez	issez	ez
For **ils; elles**	ent	issent	ent

Example: You want to say my sisters like pop music. First, identify to like in French. That's aimer, which is a regular ER verb. The pronoun you use to replace my sisters with is they, feminine, i.e. elles.

Now, apply the rule:
1. Remove the ER from aimer. This gives you the stem **aim-**
2. Check the grid. You need the first column, as it deals with ER verbs.
   Read down through the list of persons until you find elles.
   You need to add **–ent** to the stem.
   ⇝ mes sœurs **aim-** + **-ent** la musique pop = mes sœurs aiment la musique pop.

Examples: je regarde; tu choisis; elle attend; nous vendons; vous adorez; ils grandissent

A few spelling exceptions
1. When the verb ends in –ger, the nous form ending is –eons, e.g. nous mangeons. That's to keep the soft sound of that g.
The letter g is *hard* when it is followed by a, o or u, e.g. le golf, la gare and **soft** when followed by e or i. That's why there is a u in words like guitar/la guitare. It would begin like giraffe otherwise.

2. For the same reason, verbs ending in –cer keep that soft s sound by using a ç in front of the –ons ending, e.g. nous commençons.

3. Verbs ending in –yer only keep that y with the nous and vous forms. All the other persons use i instead, e.g. envoyer ⇝ j'envoie/tu envoies but nous envoyons/vous envoyez.

4. Some verbs play fast and loose with accents:
Some verbs with no accents in the **infinitive** have them in the **present tense**, but not with each person:
acheter ⇝ j'achète, tu achètes, il achète; nous achetons; vous achetez; ils achètent
se lever ⇝ je me lève ; tu te lèves ; il se lève ; nous nous levons ; vous vous levez ; ils se lèvent
Verbs with acute accents in the infinitive don't always keep those accents *acute*:
préférer ⇝ je préfère; tu préfères; il préfère; nous préférons; vous préférez; ils préfèrent

Complete French Grammar: Part 1

Irregular verbs: The Famous Five in the present tense

	AVOIR	ETRE	ALLER	FAIRE	PRENDRE
With je or j'	ai	suis	vais	fais	prends
With tu	as	es	vas	fais	prends
With il; elle; ce; ça; on	a	est	va	fait	prend
With nous	avons	sommes	allons	faisons	prenons
With vous	avez	êtes	allez	faites	prenez
With ils; elles	ont	sont	vont	font	prennent

Examples: tu prends; j'ai; ils vont; ça va; nous sommes

EXERCICES

1. Translate the following phrases into French. All the verbs are regular.
(a) She chooses (to choose = choisir) _____
(b) We're playing (to play = jouer) – Give two ways of saying this. _____
_____
(c) The boys are singing (to sing = chanter) _____
(d) Do you like..? (to like = aimer) – use the casual *you*. _____
(e) He waits (to wait = attendre) _____
(f) The little girls are growing up (to grow up = grandir) _____
_____

(g) You sell … (to sell = vendre) – use the polite *you*. _____
(h) I wash (myself) (to wash = se laver)* _____

*Se laver is a reflexive verb, like s'appeler. Remember, most reflexive verbs are regular ER verbs. The only difference is the reflexive pronoun that has to be added, e.g. tu *te* réveilles. See page 24.

Chapter 6: Verbs

2. Match the subject to a suitable irregular verb, then **finish the sentence** yourself and say what it means, e.g. *je + fais du français* = I do French/I am doing French.

Paul	vais
Mes amis	est
La souris	vas
Elles	prend
Marilyn et moi	font
Tu	sont
Toi et ta mère	avons
Je	êtes

(a) _____
(b) _____
(c) _____
(d) _____
(e) _____
(f) _____
(g) _____
(h) _____

3. In the following sentences, **fill in the gaps** with a suitable regular or irregular verb in the **present tense**. Then **translate each sentence into English**:
(a) Mes voisins _____ anglais.
(b) J' _____ trois chiens.
(c) Mes stylos _____ dans ma trousse.
(d) On _____ du chocolat.
(e) Vous _____ le bus ?

(a) _____
(b) _____
(c) _____
(d) _____
(e) _____

The Present Participle

First, let's see what a present participle is in English.
Look at the following example:

John likes playing cards.

There are two words in the verbal group in this sentence: **likes** + **playing**.
These two verbs have different meanings and the second verb ends in *-ing*. This second verb is a **present participle** in English.

Complete French Grammar: Part 1

The **present participle** in English can also be used after prepositions such as by, e.g. By leaving early, we'll be in Montpellier before twelve.

The **present participle** in French behaves a bit differently.
In the sentence John likes playing cards, the French use an infinitive, not a present participle, for the second verb, e.g. John likes playing cards = John aime jouer aux cartes.
Basically, if you can replace the verb ending in -ing (e.g. playing) with a verb starting with to... in English, you will use an **infinitive** in the French translation,
e.g. John likes playing/to play = John aime jouer.

However, you need to use a present participle in French when you use a verb with en (= by, on/upon or whilst).

Examples:
Tu réussiras en travaillant dur = You will succeed by working hard.
En arrivant, on a pris le Métro = On arriving, we took the Métro.
Je suis tombé en jouant au hockey = I fell whilst playing hockey.

You can see how the **present participle** could be really useful (and impressive!) in your written work.

The way to form the present participle is to look at the nous form of any verb in the **present tense** (**ER**, **IR** or **RE**) and remove the –ons ending. This gives the stem, to which you add – ant.

Example: To translate playing.
we play = nous jouons
Remove the –ons to get the stem ⇾ jou-
Add –ant ⇾ jou- + -ant = jouant
jouant = playing

(Three exceptions: being = étant; having = ayant; knowing = sachant)

Sometimes, there is a need for the **present participle** in French, but not in English. English is a wonderfully elastic language where you can say things like, he ran out of the room. The French language is not so nimble and that sentence in French has to be he went/came out of the room *running*. To express that, you need the **present participle**. ⇾ il est sorti de la pièce en courant.

In English and in French, the **present participle** is also used to create **adjectives** out of verbs, e.g. charming comes from to charm; in French, charmant comes from charmer. However, like all adjectives in French, present participles used as adjectives agree with their noun.

Example: un film intéressant/une histoire intéressante

Note
Remember that in English, not all verbs ending in -ing are **present participles**.
Look at this example: John is playing cards.
You cannot replace playing with to play in the example.

The verbal group **is playing** is in the **present tense** and the sentence translates into French as, John joue aux cartes. You do not translate the is nor the playing separately.

EXERCICES

Translate the following sentences into French:
(a) I saw Marie when on my way (=while going) to school.   (to go = aller)
(b) I went in by opening the door.   (to open = ouvrir)
(c) I went in shouting.   (to shout = crier)
(d) He listens to music whilst waiting for the bus.   (to wait for = attendre)
(e) She broke her leg whilst skiing.   (to ski = faire du ski)

(a) _____
(b) _____
(c) _____
(d) _____
(e) _____

The Passé Composé

Also known as the **perfect**, the **passé composé** is the tense you use to say **what happened**. You use it to talk about something that happened just once in the past (e.g. I went to the cinema, I have eaten an apple), rather than something you regularly used to do in the past.

The **passé composé** means composed past, so remember you will need to combine TWO words.

The first word of the **passé composé** is called the **auxiliary**. It is either avoir or être in their **present tense** forms.
The second word is called the **past participle**. It carries all the meaning, as in English.
For example, I have done that.
Have = the auxiliary. Done = the **past participle**.
In French, you will always need **both** the auxiliary and the past participle.

Complete French Grammar: Part 1

First, find out the **infinitive** (= verb itself as in To do) of the verb you want to use. Then, you need to find out which **auxiliary** to use, so ask yourself the following questions:

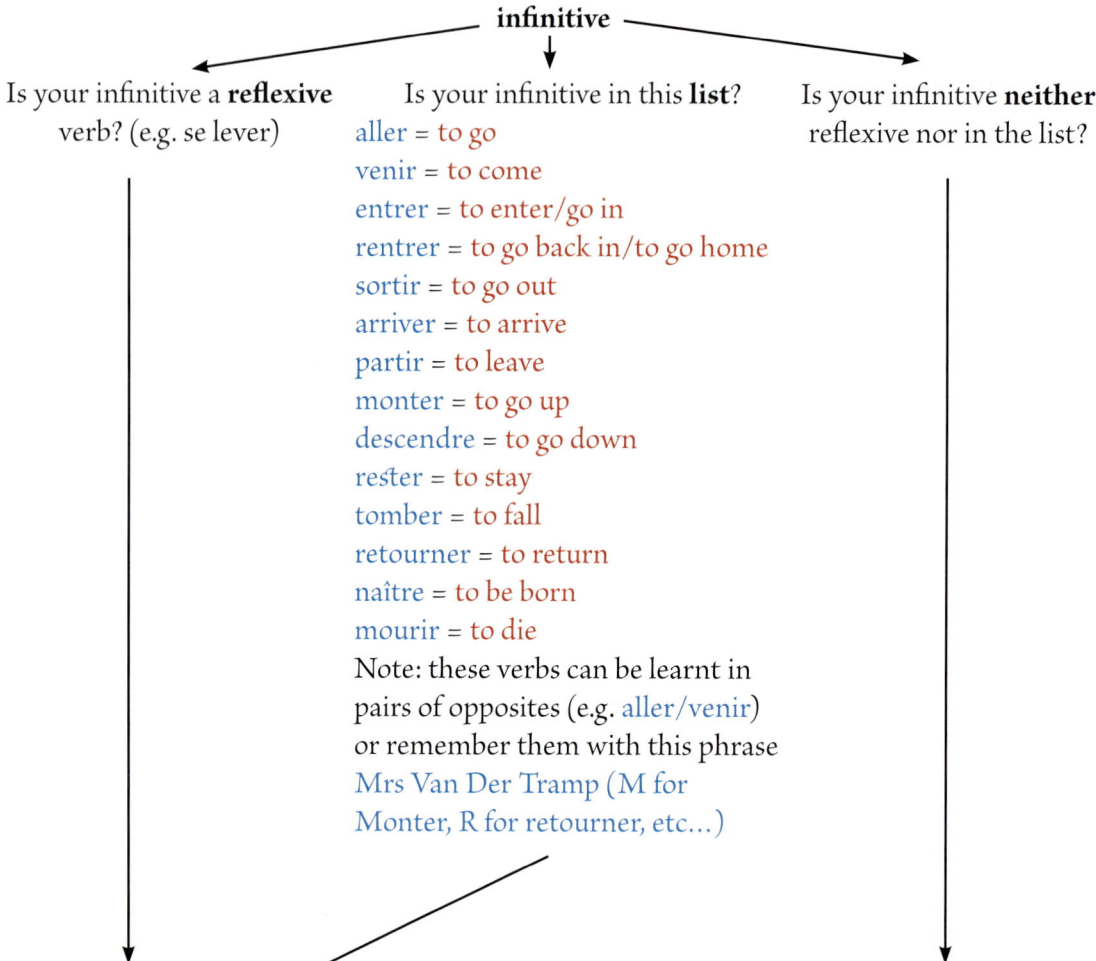

infinitive

Is your infinitive a **reflexive** verb? (e.g. se lever)

Is your infinitive in this **list**?
aller = to go
venir = to come
entrer = to enter/go in
rentrer = to go back in/to go home
sortir = to go out
arriver = to arrive
partir = to leave
monter = to go up
descendre = to go down
rester = to stay
tomber = to fall
retourner = to return
naître = to be born
mourir = to die
Note: these verbs can be learnt in pairs of opposites (e.g. aller/venir) or remember them with this phrase Mrs Van Der Tramp (M for Monter, R for retourner, etc...)

Is your infinitive **neither** reflexive nor in the list?

You will need one of these as your first word (= **auxiliary**):

(je) suis   (this is the
(tu) es   être verb)
(il/elle/on) est
(nous) sommes
(vous) êtes
(ils/elles) sont

You will need one of these as your first word (=**auxiliary**):

(j') ai   (this is the
(tu) as   avoir verb)
(il/elle/on) a
(nous) avons
(vous) avez
(ils/elles) ont

Note: Don't forget the reflexive bit, e.g. je me suis, if needed.

Chapter 6: Verbs

Now you need a second word, the **past participle**, so go back to your original verb in the infinitive and ask yourself these questions:

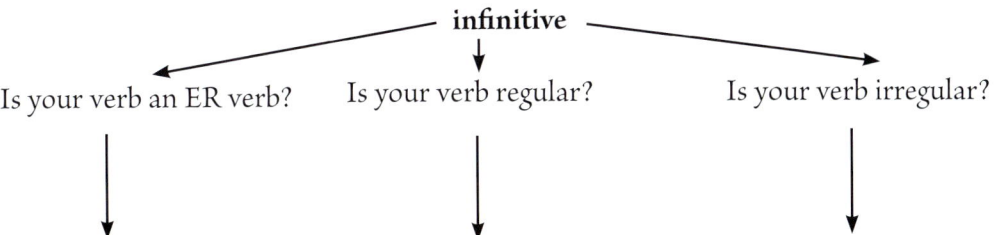

Is your verb an ER verb?	Is your verb regular?	Is your verb irregular?
To get your second word (= **past participle**), remove the ER at the end of your verb and replace it with é e.g. jouer → joué	To get your second word (=**past participle**), follow this rule: If your verb is a regular IR verb, replace the IR with i e.g. finir → fini If your verb is a regular RE verb, replace the RE with u e.g. vendre → vendu	If your verb is irregular, you can't apply any rule. You must learn the list of irregular past participles. Here is a list of common irregular past participles:

bu = drunk   mort = died / dead
cru = believed
couru = run   né = born
dit = said   ouvert = opened
dormi = slept   parti = left
dû = had to   pris = taken
eu = had/got   pu = been able to
écrit = written   reçu = received
été = been   ri = laughed
fait = done/made   sorti = gone out
lu = read   vu = seen
mis = put   voulu = wanted

Now, put your first word (**auxiliary**) and your second word (**past participle**) together and you have a **passé composé**.
Example: You want to say I visited the Louvre and I saw the Mona Lisa. First, to visit is visiter and to see is voir.
Visiter is not reflexive (it's not se visiter) and it's not in the Mrs Van Der Tramp list, so we will need avoir as the **auxiliary**. The person (i.e. the subject of the verb) you want is I so you look for the je form in the **avoir** list and you find j'ai. Visiter is an ER verb so you remove the ER and replace it with é, this gives you visité. Put the two together and you get: **j'ai visité**.
Now, do the same with voir. It's not reflexive, it's not in the Mrs Van Der Tramp list so it's an avoir verb again. You start with j'ai again. Voir, however, is irregular so consult the irregular **past participles** list. There, you look for seen and you find vu. Put the two together and you get: **j'ai vu**.
The whole sentence is: **J'ai visité le Louvre et j'ai vu la Joconde** (la Joconde is what the French call the Mona Lisa.)

Complete French Grammar: Part 1

One last thing to take into account: if your auxiliary is être, your **past participle** will have to agree with the subject, i.e. take an e for the feminine singular, s for masculine and mixed plurals and es for feminine plurals.

Example: Julie says je suis allée
         Thomas and Marc say nous sommes allés
         Julie and Marc say nous sommes allés also
         Julie and Florence say nous sommes allées.

When on is used as a casual nous, the past participle also agrees, e.g. on est parti(e)s.

EXERCICES

1. Fill in the gaps with the missing **auxiliary**:
(a) Tu _____ regardé la télé hier soir?
(b) On _____ partis à huit heures.
(c) Ils _____ vu la Joconde au Louvre.
(d) Je _____ descendue dans le sud de la France.
(e) Elle _____ joué au tennis avec son frère.

2. Fill in the gaps with a suitable **past participle**:
(a) Nous avons _____ le film.
(b) Il est _____ en ville.
(c) Vous avez _____ une lettre.
(d) J'ai _____ un garçon sympa en colonie de vacances.
(e) Elles sont _____ ce matin.

3. Match an item from Column A to an item from Column B to make five sentences.

A	B
Elle a	pris le train
Nous sommes	joué au foot
Tu as	monté dans l'avion
Il est	fini tes devoirs
Vous avez	arrivés en retard

(a) _____
(b) _____
(c) _____
(d) _____
(e) _____

The Imperfect

The expressions in the **imperfect** listed below are the most common.
It is worth learning these expressions as you will meet them (and write/say them) yourself.
J'étais = I was; J'avais = I had/I used to have; C'était = it was; Il y avait = there was;
Il faisait = the weather was; Il pleuvait = it was raining

Chapter 6: Verbs

However, the **imperfect** is the *other* important past tense. Whereas the **passé composé** deals with what happened, the **imperfect** deals **with what was happening, what used to happen** and **how things were**. When it comes to telling a good story about something that has already happened, you will need both tenses.

How to Form the Imperfect

The way to form the **imperfect** is to identify the nous form of your verb in the **present tense** and remove the –ons ending (and the nous!). This gives you the **stem**.

To that stem, you will need to **add the correct ending**. The good news is that you use the same endings for an ER verb, an IR verb or an RE verb.

	Add this ending:
For je or j'	ais
For tu	ais
For il; elle; ce; ça; on	ait
For nous	ions
For vous	iez
For ils; elles	aient

Examples: You want to say I was watching TV. The verb to watch is regarder. You need we watch to find the stem → nous regardons. Remove the –ons. This gives the stem regard-
Check the grid for the correct ending. You need the I form, that's je in French, so the ending is –ais.
Put the two together: je regard- + -ais → je regardais la télé.
You will notice that we did not translate the verb literally. There is no was and no watching. In fact, je regardais could mean I was watching or I used to watch. You need to know the context to know which one it means in English.
If you want to say it was, you need the verb être which has an exceptional stem. You need to use ét-.
Check the grid for the correct ending. It is ce, so you'll need the ending –ait.
Put everything together and you get ce + ét- + -ait → c'était. (ce will become c' because était starts with a vowel) **Examples:** j'aimais; tu regardais; vous alliez; ils faisaient

EXERCICES

Put the verbs in brackets into the imperfect:

(a) Ils (aller) souvent au cinéma. _____
(b) Je (regarder) la télé quand Mathilde est arrivée. _____
(c) Vous (finir) de manger? _____
(d) Nous (étudier) le Latin quand j' (être) jeune. Note: the stem of étudier is étudi-, so yes, you'll need to write the letter **i** twice! _____
(e) Il y (avoir) du brouillard sur la route. _____

Complete French Grammar: Part 1

Clash of the Titans: Passé Composé versus Imperfect

The main difficulty with these two past tenses is that they can occur in the same sentence. You need to be careful or your story could be very different to the one you intended to tell! Compare these two examples:

(a) Le téléphone a sonné quand je prenais un bain.
(b) Le téléphone a sonné quand j'ai pris un bain.

Example (a) means that the phone rang when *I was taking* a bath. In other words, I was already covered in suds when the phone rang.

Example (b) means that the phone rang when *I took* a bath. It sounds as if the phone waited for me to get in the bath before ringing!

This shows that you must decide which of the two tenses to use. It all depends on what you mean.

Look at these examples:

(a) il pleuvait = it was raining
(b) il a plu = it rained

In example (a), you're giving more of a description, it implies the rain was falling for a while.

In example (b), you're merely stating the fact that it rained, you're not passing judgement.

In most cases, there will be a clear choice to make between the two tenses.

To help you with that, have a look at the following checklist:

A
Are you being **factual, objective,** and saying **merely what happened?** That's the **passé composé**, e.g. Je suis allé en ville: I went into town

B
Are you referring to a **once-off event in the past?** That's also the **passé composé**, e.g. J'ai recontré le Président: I met the President

C
Are you **setting the scene** by saying **what you were doing** when something else happened? That's the **imperfect**, e.g. Je regardais la télé quand tu es arrivé: I was watching TV when you arrived

D
Are you referring to something you **used to do**, concentrating on the length or the **repetitive aspect** of the action and not just the fact that you did it? That's the **imperfect** e.g. J'aimais bien ce groupe mais plus maintenant: I used to like this band but not anymore

E
Are you offering an **opinion** or a **description**, in other words, are you being **subjective?** That's the **imperfect**, too, e.g. C'était super, il y avait plein de choses à faire: It was brilliant, there was lots to do

F
For these reasons, the **passé composé** carries a story forward but the **imperfect** doesn't, e.g. il faisait beau (**imperfect**), j'ai fait une promenade (**passé composé**): the weather was good (the story is static), I went for a walk (the story moves forward). You can think of it as a film: the **imperfect** is everything in the background, the **passé composé** is the action.

Chapter 6: Verbs

Here are two stories told using both the **passé composé** and the **imperfect**. The first one clearly illustrates the contrast between what **used to be** the case and **what happened** next:

Story 1

Quand j'**étais** plus jeune, j'**habitais** en Angleterre. Mon père **travaillait** pour une compagnie anglaise. On **avait** un appartement à Londres, c'**était** chouette! Il y a trois ans, on **a déménagé** et on **est venus** habiter ici. On **a acheté** une grande maison à la campagne et ça, c'est bien aussi!

Translation

When I was younger, I used to live in England. My father was working for an English company. We had/used to have an apartment in London, it was great! Three years ago, we moved and we came to live here. We bought a big house in the country and that's great too!

- J'étais = I was

  J'ai été = I have been would not work here as it does not make sense to say I have been young.

  (Note: Generally speaking, être is more likely to be used in the **imperfect** than in the **passé composé**.)

- J'habitais en… = I lived in …/I used to live in …

  In this case, we are setting the scene so I used to live (i.e. the **imperfect**) is the best translation as it implies that it was something you did for a while (i.e. you lived there for a while). I lived can be translated from English into French as j'ai habité if you want to state the fact that at one time, you lived in .. (e.g. I have lived in many different countries).

- Mon père travaillait = My father used to work/was working

  We're still setting the scene so we're using the **imperfect**. It's an explanation as to why they lived in England. Mon père a travaillé would not be right here as it would mean my father has worked.

- On avait = We had/we used to have

  If the verb phrase on a eu had been used, it would actually change the story because avoir in the **passé composé** is more likely to mean to get than to have, i.e. on a eu = we got. So on avait is the **imperfect**.

- C'était = it was

  This is one of the useful phrases in the **imperfect** given to you at the beginning of this section. It's used to give all kinds of opinions, e.g. c'était nul = it was rubbish, and other bits of background information, e.g. c'était l'hiver = it was winter. It's the past version of c'est, so it is very useful. Less useful, but still an option, is the phrase ça a été = it has been.

- On a déménagé = We moved (house)

  This is the **passé composé** because we're now talking about what happened, i.e something that happened once. As the house move happened once and was a completed action, on déménageait (**imperfect**) would not work here as it means either we were moving or we used to move.

- On est venus = We came

  Again, this is what happened just once. **Passé composé.** It doesn't suit the story to say on venait = we were coming/we used to come (**imperfect**).

- On a acheté = We bought

  This is clearly a once-off event that happened in the past, so it has to be **passé composé**. On achetait (**imperfect**) means we used to buy or we were buying, neither of which suits our story.

Complete French Grammar: Part 1

Here is another story in which the two tenses mix more freely:

Story 2

Samedi dernier, j'**étais** en ville pour faire quelques courses quand tout à coup, j'**ai entendu** une femme crier « Au voleur! Il m'a volé mon sac! » **J'ai vu** un jeune homme qui **s'enfuyait**. Il **était** grand et il **courait** vite. À un moment donné, un homme, qui **avait** de bons réflexes, lui a **fait** un croche-pied et le voleur **est tombé** par terre. Il **s'est relevé** très vite et il **est reparti** en laissant le sac derrière lui. La dame **était** très contente de retrouver son sac parce qu'**il y avait** tous ses papiers et ses cartes bancaires dedans. Le voleur, lui, **n'a pas été retrouvé!**

Translation

Last Saturday, I was in town to do some shopping when suddenly, I heard a woman scream 'Stop, thief! He stole my bag!' I saw a young man who was running away. He was tall and he was running fast. At one point, a man who had good reflexes tripped him up and the robber fell to the ground. He got back up quickly and he set off again leaving the bag behind. The lady was very happy to get her bag back because she had (there was) all her papers and bank cards inside. (As for) the robber, he has not been found again!

- J'étais = I was We're setting the scene. **Imperfect**
- J'ai entendu = I heard This is a once-off event in the past, we're saying simply what happened. So that's **passé composé**.
- J'ai vu = I saw This is a once-off event in the past, it's what happened. Again, that's **passé composé**.
- (qui) s'enfuyait = (who) was running away This says that the young man had probably started running before our writer saw him and kept running (until he was tripped up in fact!). **Imperfect** If you say j'ai vu un jeune home qui s'est enfui, you're saying I saw a young man who ran away. This sounds as if he ran away as soon as you looked at him. This does not have the same meaning as I saw a young man who was running away.
- Il était = he was You can't really say he has been tall, (il a été), can you?! **Imperfect**
- Il courait = he was running Again, that's part of the description. We're not saying he ran (il a couru). **Imperfect**
- (qui) avait = (who) had That's another description. Descriptions require the **imperfect**.
- (un homme) a fait = (a man) did (faire un croche-pied à quelqu'un = to trip somebody up) This is, luckily perhaps for the young man, a once-off event in the past, we're stating what happened. A one-off event = the **passé composé**.
- Le voleur est tombé = the robber fell/il s'est relevé = he got back up again/il est reparti = he set off again All these relate what happened. **Passé composé** (Note: Adding re- to the start of a verb can give the meaning of again, e.g. partir → repartir; commencer → recommencer)
- La dame était = the lady was This is a description. **Imperfect**
Note the two words used in the extract to refer to the poor victim: la femme = the woman; la dame = the woman/the lady, a bit more friendly than la femme.

Chapter 6: Verbs

- **Il y avait** = there was
  This is another of the essential expressions in the **Imperfect**. You use it to describe plenty of things, e.g. il y avait du vent = it was windy (there was a lot of wind); il y avait beaucoup de monde au concert = the concert was packed (there were a lot of people at the concert).

- **Le voleur n'a pas été retrouvé** = the robber was not found again
  We're stating a fact, here. **Passé composé**
  Note the structures used: as you can see, it's in the **negative**, using ne and pas. To say he has been found, you'd write il a été retrouvé. But look more closely and you'll see that there are three words used for this **passé composé**. That's because the phrase is in the **passive voice**. The passive voice in French is formed much like in English: the verb être is used in various tenses, with a past participle, e.g. elle sera invitée = she will be invited.

EXERCICES

1. **Choose** between the **passé composé** and the **imperfect** in the following sentences and **explain** your choice.
   (a) **J'ai vu/Je voyais** un bon film hier soir. _____
   (b) On est allés à la plage mais **il a plu/il pleuvait**. _____
   (c) Avant, **ils ont joué/ils jouaient** au rugby, mais **ils ont arrêté/ils arrêtaient**. _____
   (d) **Tu as été/Tu étais** malade ? _____
   (e) **Il y a eu /il y avait** un accident sur l'autoroute A4 dimanche. _____

2. **Translate** the following sentences into French:
   (a) I fell when I was playing basket ball.
   (b) We went to a music festival, there were a lot of people there and we had a great time! (Note: To have a great time is bien s'amuser. The word bien comes after the verb in one word tenses [e.g. je m'amuse bien, present tense] and after the first verb in constructions using more than one verb [e.g. je vais bien m'amuser, immediate future].)
   (c) He used to take his car to go to work, but last year, he started taking the bus. (Note: to start doing something is commencer à + infinitive.)
   (d) I saw the robber! He was fat, he had grey hair and he was wearing a blue jacket.
   (e) My parents and I were very sad when you left.

   (a) _____
   (b) _____
   (c) _____
   (d) _____
   (e) _____

Complete French Grammar: Part 1

The Immediate Past
This is not really a tense but a verb construction. It is very easy to use and will express that you have *just* done something. You use the verb **venir** in the **present tense** (be careful, venir is irregular), you add **de** and then your **infinitive**.

Example: You want to say I've just finished my exams.
The verb **venir** in the **present tense** with je is **je viens; de** comes next; then the verb to finish (the infinitive) which is **finir**.

Je viens de finir mes examens.

The interesting point with this structure is that you do not use a past tense. All you need to know is venir in the **present tense** and the infinitive of the verb you're using. Of course, on the downside, it can only be used for very recent events.

EXERCICES

Translate the following sentences into French:
(a) We've just finished our exams.
(b) She's just bought a new car.
(c) They've just left.
(d) Have you just arrived?
(e) I've just seen a great film.

The Future
This is the tense you use to say you **will** do something. It is the tense you must use in **formal letters**.
Unlike English, there is no word for **will** in French to show the verb is in the future. Instead you have to change the verb just like you do for other tenses.
The good news is that **all verbs** use the same set of **endings**:

	Add this ending:
For **je or j'**	ai
For **tu**	as
For **il; elle; ce; ça; on**	a
For **nous**	ons
For **vous**	ez
For **ils ; elles**	ont

Note: Did you notice that those endings look very like the verb avoir in the **present tense**? That might help you to remember them.

Chapter 6: Verbs

To get the **stem**, you need to know whether your verb is **regular** or **irregular**:
Regular verb stem:
You will actually use the full infinitive, e.g. manger. The only part you remove is the e of RE verbs because otherwise you'd have too many vowels together.
And watch out for acheter which will have a grave accent on the first e, e.g. j'ach**è**terai.

Irregular verb stem:
    We're back to learning a list. Here are a few common irregular stems:
    avoir → **aur-**
    être → **ser-**
    aller → **ir-**
    faire → **fer-**
    prendre → **prendr-**
    envoyer → **enverr-**
    pouvoir → **pourr-**
    devoir → **devr-**
    vouloir → **voudr-**
    voir → **verr-**

Note: All stems in the future end in r.

Now, you put the **stem** and the **ending** together to get the future tense of the verb you want to use.

Examples:
You want to say I will travel. The verb to travel is voyager. It is a regular verb so you will keep the full infinitive. The person you're using is je so the ending you need is **–ai**.
I will travel → je + voyager- + -ai → je voyagerai

You now want to say we will go. To go is aller, which is irregular. Check the list of irregular stems and you find that for aller, you need the stem ir-. Next, you need to decide whether you're using on or nous for we. The on ending is –a and the nous ending is –ons.
We will go → (i) on + ir- + -a → on ira   (ii) nous + ir- + -ons → nous irons

EXERCICES

Put the verbs in brackets into the Future:
(a) Ils (faire) la vaisselle plus tard. _____
(b) On (pouvoir) faire du bateau. _____
(c) Tu (aller) chez tes grands-parents cet été? _____
(d) Je te (téléphoner) ce soir, ok ? _____
(e) Elle (avoir) 16 ans en juillet. _____

Note: In English, when you say something like *I will phone you when I arrive*, oddly enough the second verb (i.e. *arrive*) is in the **present tense**. The French don't find that logical, so you will need to put both verbs into the **future**.
I will phone you when I arrive → je te téléphone*rai* quand j'arrive*rai*.

The Immediate Future

Like its partner the **immediate past**, this is not a tense but a very useful verb construction. As in English, you use *aller* in the **present tense** and you add any infinitive you like to that, e.g. *You are going to learn* = tu vas apprendre.
It is very handy in **informal letter** writing when you can't remember the **future**, though it is best to use it to describe events that are going to happen shortly or events that you're looking forward to.

Example: You want to say *she's going to sing*. Check the verb *aller* in the **present tense** and find the *she* form → elle va. The verb *to sing* is *chanter*, keep it in the **infinitive**. Put the two together. *She's going to sing* → elle va + chanter = elle va chanter

EXERCICES

Translate the following sentences into French:
(a) We're going to play soccer this afternoon.
(b) Are you going to travel by boat?
(c) I'm going to revise for my exams.
(d) My cousins are going to go to Austria in January.
(e) Nadège is going to be 15. (Careful!)
(a) _____
(b) _____
(c) _____
(d) _____
(e) _____

The Conditional

This is what you use to say you **would** do something. It implies a **condition**, hence its name. When you say *I could do that*, there is an **if** hiding somewhere, such as **if** I had the time or **if** I was fitter! Again, there is no word for **would** in French so you will have to change the verb to make it clear it's in the **conditional**. To form the **conditional**, you need the **stems** of the **future** and the **endings** of the **imperfect**:

Full infinitive (without the E of RE verbs)
or   +
Irregular stem

ais
ais
ait
ions
iez
aient

Chapter 6: Verbs

Example: You want to say we could … The infinitive of could is to be able to.
That's the verb pouvoir, which is irregular. Its stem in the Future is pourr-.
The person you need is we so you can choose to use on or nous. The ending for on is –ait and the ending for nous is –ions.
We could … ↦ (i) on + pourr- + -ait = on pourrait   (ii) nous + pourr- + -ions = nous pourrions

This is a useful phrase for letter writing, such as when you're asked to say what your penpal and you could do during his/her stay, e.g. we could visit the castle = on pourrait visiter le château. It's also used in the phrase we could go and collect you = on pourrait aller te chercher.

EXERCICES

Put the verb in brackets into the conditional:
(a) Tu n'(avoir) pas un stylo à me prêter? _____
(b) Je (vouloir) deux kilos de pommes, s'il vous plaît. _____
(c) Chloé (aimer) devenir actrice. _____
(d) Je suis sûr que tes profs (pouvoir) t'aider. _____
(e) Si j'étais riche, j'(acheter) une Ferrari.* _____

*You will notice that when the **condition** is expressed (if I was rich), it's in the **imperfect**.

A quick word on the **conditional** in the past, which is when you say what you would have done.
If you break down what you say in English, you get the French formation:
I would have = to have, in the **conditional** + done = the **past participle** of to do
↦ j'aurais (avoir in the **conditional**) + fait (**past participle** of faire)
Examples: she would have liked = elle aurait aimé; they would have gone = ils seraient allés

The Imperative

This is what you use to ask/tell people what to do, e.g. Listen!
It is used in **recipes**, e.g. add = ajoutez, and when getting/giving **directions**.
Example: Turn left = Tournez à gauche

You use it in **messages** or at the **end of letters**:
n'oublie pas de … = don't forget to …
téléphone-moi = phone me
envoie-moi des photos = send me some pictures
dis bonjour à tes parents = say hi to your parents
écris-moi vite = write to me soon (vite = quickly)

The thing about the **imperative** is that it has only **three persons**. Think about it: you can tell one person to listen, you can also tell a group of people to listen and finally you can say let's listen. That's it.

Complete French Grammar: Part 1

In French, this is obviously also the case. The **imperative** looks different to the other tenses because it does not **have a subject pronoun**.
Examples:
Écoute! (one person, casual); Écoutez! (one person, polite/group); Écoutons! (let's listen)

You can see from the examples that the imperative looks like the **present tense**. This is essentially what you use, but *without* the subject pronoun.

When addressing one person, casually, use the tu form of the **present tense** but remove the **s** in the case of ER verbs,
Example: tu bois (**present tense**) → Bois! (**imperative**)
                  tu parles (**present tense**) → Parle! (**imperative**)

When addressing one person politely or addressing a group of people, use the vous form of the present tense.
Example: vous prenez (**present tense**) → Prenez! (**imperative**)

When saying let's ..., use the nous form of the **present tense**
Example: nous finissons (**present tense**) → Finissons! (**imperative**)

There are only a few exceptions that you need to know:
With **avoir**, the three **imperative** forms are: **aie; ayez; ayons**
With **être**, the three **imperative** forms are: **sois; soyez; soyons**
The polite **veuillez** (from **vouloir**) is used in formal letters when asking for something to be sent to you etc, e.g. veuillez m'envoyer une brochure = please send me a brochure.

The **imperative** is often used in the **negative**. To do this, just frame the verb with the two negative parts, as you would in an ordinary sentence, e.g. n'oublie pas = don't forget; n'aie plus peur = don't be afraid anymore; ne faites jamais ça = never do that

You also have to be careful when the **imperative** is used with **object pronouns**, e.g. give me, take them etc. The pronouns you use here are: moi (me/to me); toi (you/to you); le (it/him); la (it/her); lui (to it/to him/to her); nous (us/to us); vous (you/to you); les (them); leur (to them), e.g. donne-moi; prends-les.

As you can see from the examples, the object pronoun goes directly *after* the verb. However, if you are using the **imperative in the negative with object pronouns**, moi becomes me, toi becomes te and the structure will change, e.g. don't give me = ne me donne pas; don't take them = ne les prends pas. The object pronoun is now before the verb and both words are framed by the negative expression. (A negative expression can be ne + pas but also ne + jamais, ne + plus etc).

Chapter 6: Verbs

EXERCICES

In the following sentences, **put the English phrases into French,** and then **say what the whole sentence means:**
- **(a)** (Don't forget) d' apporter un sac de couchage.
- **(b)** (Wait for me) avant d'aller à la patinoire.
- **(c)** (Let's take) la prochaine route, et (let's hope) que c'est la bonne!
- **(d)** (Be) sympa, (give me) un de tes bonbons!
- **(e)** (Turn) à gauche et après ça, (look at) les panneaux!

(a) _____
(b) _____
(c) _____
(d) _____
(e) _____

Chapter 7: ADVERBS

Adverbs are words that can change the whole meaning of a sentence. This is because they influence the verb. Compare: ils chantent *bien* = they sing well; ils chantent *mal* = they sing badly.

Many adverbs in English end in –ly. The equivalent of that –ly is –ment in French. This appears at the end of an adjective, usually in the feminine, lent/lente = slow; lente**ment** = slowly

Short adverbs usually appear next to or close to the verb within the sentence, even in the negative, but longer ones are a bit more independent:

(a) **Example** of short adverb:
Il court **vite** = he runs fast; il ne court pas **vite** = he does not run fast
(b) **Example** of longer adverb:
généralement, on va chez ma tante à Pâques
or on va **généralement** chez ma tante à Pâques
or even on va chez ma tante à Pâques, **généralement** =
we usually go to my aunt's at Easter

Here is a list of **useful adverbs**:
bien = well, e.g. je vais bien = I am well
mal = badly, e.g. j'ai mal dormi = I slept badly
mieux = better, e.g. ma mère va mieux = my mother is better
tôt = early, e.g. je me lève tôt = I get up early
tard = late, e.g. je me suis levé tard = I got up late
vite = fast, e.g. le TGV va vite = the TGV train goes fast
rapidement = quickly, rapidly, e.g. on a mangé rapidement = we ate quickly
bientôt = soon, e.g. écris-moi bientôt = write to me soon
déjà = already, e.g. j'ai déjà vu ce film = I've seen this film already
beaucoup = a lot, e.g. j'aime beaucoup les légumes = I like vegetables a lot
ensemble = together, e.g. on a voyagé ensemble = we travelled together
ensuite = then, e.g. on ira à Marseille et ensuite à Nice =
We will go to Marseille and then to Nice.
encore = again, once more, e.g. tu es encore tombé? = did you fall again?
(Note: to express to do something again, re- is added to the verb instead of using encore, e.g. on se reverra bientôt = we will see each other again soon.
heureusement = fortunately, e.g. il a eu son permis, heureusement =
he got his driving licence, fortunately
malheureusement = unfortunately, e.g. malheureusement, il s'est cassé la jambe = unfortunately, he broke his leg

Chapter 7: Adverbs

normalement = normally; usually; all things going well, e.g. normalement, on arrivera à midi = all things going well, we will arrive at midday
partout = everywhere, e.g. il a regardé partout = he looked everywhere
nulle part = nowhere, e.g. je ne suis allé nulle part ce weekend = I went nowhere this weekend
ailleurs = elsewhere, e.g. je l'ai acheté ailleurs = I bought it elsewhere
facilement = easily, e.g. j'ai ouvert la boîte facilement = I opened the tin easily
toujours = always; still, e.g. je joue toujours = I always play or I still play
(Note: another word for still is encore, as in tu as encore faim? = are you still hungry?)
jamais = never, e.g. tu ne m'écoutes jamais! = you never listen to me!
(Note that **jamais plus/plus jamais** means never again, e.g. je n'irai jamais plus dans ce magasin = I will never go back to that shop)
vraiment = really, truly, e.g. tu aimes vraiment ce film? = do you really like this film?
(Note: **très, trop, assez, plus, moins, ici, là, devant, derrière** are also adverbs.)

Here are a few expressions that can be used as adverbs:
d'abord = firstly, e.g. d'abord le fromage, ensuite le dessert!= first(ly), the cheese, then dessert!
d'habitude = usually, e.g. d'habitude, je commence à neuf heures = I usually start at nine
cher + verb = a lot of money, e.g. ça coûte cher = it costs a lot of money; il a payé cher = he paid a lot of money (or even the more figurative he paid dearly)
fort = strongly; loudly, e.g. ce fromage sent fort = this cheese is smelly (smells strongly); le vent souffle fort = the wind is strong (blows strongly); elle parle fort = she's loud (speaks loudly)
bien sûr = of course, e.g. j'ai gagné, bien sûr! = I won, of course!
peut-être = maybe, e.g. on ira peut-être à Lyon cet été = we will maybe go to Lyon this summer

EXERCICES

Translate the following sentences into French:
(a) He plays soccer really well.
(b) We're always tired during the week but never at the weekend!
(c) Unfortunately, he speaks badly and fast.
(d) They got up early and they went to town together.
(e) Usually, I eat in the cafeteria; it doesn't cost too much money.

(a) _____
(b) _____
(c) _____
(d) _____
(e) _____

Part 2: Going Further
Deuxième Partie - Approfondissement

Welcome to Part Two of your Complete French Grammar.
Part One introduced you to the basics and now, in theory, you are ready to tackle more challenging issues, such as the subjunctive tense and the passive voice!

Chapter 8: MORE TENSES

PERSONS

We will start with a word about the term **person**, used in many grammar books.

When you speak French, your verb changes according to the subject you're using, i.e. the verb form with je is likely to be very different from the nous form.
What makes it a little difficult in French is that there are up to **six** different verb forms in any given tense, according to the **person** you're using. When you look at irregular verb lists, you can see this clearly.
The reason there are only (!) six lines in irregular verb lists is that you can group some pronouns together; the verb form is the same with all the pronouns in the same **person** group.

Here is how it goes for **subject pronouns:**

First person singular	– première personne du singulier	= je or j'
Second person singular	– deuxième personne du singulier	= tu
Third person singular	– troisième personne du singulier	= il; elle; ce; ça; on
First person plural	– première personne du pluriel	= nous
Second person plural	– deuxième personne du pluriel	= vous
Third person plural	– troisième personne du pluriel	= ils; elles

An interesting conclusion to be drawn from this system is that since on (= casual we) and il (= he) are in the same **person** group, the on verb form will be the same as the il verb form, two for the price of one!

Note: Some grammar books will use this way of grouping all pronouns (e.g. object pronouns), not just I, you, he, she, etc.

Chapter 8: More Tenses

VERBS: THEIR MOODS AND TENSES

Strictly speaking, there are **moods** (modes) and within those moods, there are **tenses** (temps). You remember the conditional? That's when you say **would**. Well, it's usually referred to as a tense but, in fact, it's a mood. There is more than one tense within the conditional: compare I would go to I would have gone.
I would go (= j'irais) is the present conditional and I would have gone (= je serais allé) is the past conditional.

The mood we use most is the **Indicative Mood** (le mode indicatif), which contains amongst others the present, the perfect/passé composé, the imperfect, and the future. So if you see a reference to le présent de l'indicatif, it is just the humble present tense.

The complete list of **indicative tenses** is:
Le présent (present); le passé composé (perfect); l'imparfait (imperfect); le plus-que-parfait (pluperfect); le passé simple (past historic); le passé antérieur (past anterior); le futur simple (future); le futur antérieur (future perfect).

We covered the present, the passé composé, the imperfect and the future in Part One. We will have a look at three more in Part Two: the **plus-que-parfait**; the **passé simple** and the **futur antérieur**.

LE PLUS-QUE-PARFAIT – PLUPERFECT

This is the past form of the passé composé! In other words, it expresses an event that had happened *before* something else happened, e.g. il **avait fini** son examen quand la cloche *a sonné* = he **had finished** his exam when the bell *rang*. You can see that la cloche a sonné is in the passé composé. Because he had finished his exam *before* the bell rang, you need the pluperfect to express that fact. If you wrote *il a fini son examen quand la cloche a sonné*, with the two verbs in the passé composé, it would mean that he finished his exam just when the bell rang – the two events coincided, he was cutting it a bit fine!

The pluperfect can also be used **with the imperfect,** e.g. Quand il **avait lu** le journal, il me le *donnait* = When he had read the newspaper, he used to give it to me.
It can also partner **the past conditional**, e.g. Si j'**avais eu** le temps, je *serais allé* au marché = If I had had the time, I would have gone to the market.

To conjugate a verb in the plus-que-parfait, you need to know its passé composé/perfect tense form. All you need to do is put the auxiliary (avoir or être) in the *imperfect* instead of the present. You do the same in English by replacing have with had. You then add the past participle, e.g. ils sont allés (= they have gone; passé composé) → ils étaient allés (= they had gone; pluperfect).
Avoir in the imperfect: j'avais; tu avais; il avait; nous avions; vous aviez; ils avaient
Être in the imperfect: j'étais; tu étais; il était; nous étions; vous étiez; ils étaient

Complete French Grammar: Part 2

EXERCICES

1. Put the following verbs which are in the passé composé into the **pluperfect:**
    - J'ai joué
    - Ils ont vu
    - Nous sommes partis
    - Tu as mangé
    - Vous êtes arrivés
    - Elle a perdu

2. Decide whether the verb in brackets should be **in the pluperfect or not**, then put that verb into the **correct tense and person**. All these events take place in the past.
    - **(a)** Je (réaliser) que je (lire) ce livre récemment.
    - **(b)** Quand il (finir) ses devoirs, il (regarder) un peu la télé.
    - **(c)** Si on (savoir), on (partir) plus tôt.
    - **(d)** Ils (sortir) quand nous (passer) chez eux.

We are now going to see another tense in the indicative mood, called the **passé simple** or past historic in English.

LE PASSÉ SIMPLE – PAST HISTORIC

The **passé simple/past historic** is a formal past tense used in writing instead of the passé composé. It is seen as too formal to be spoken or even used in letters; it is the tense of biographies, novels, articles etc.

It is quite distinctive in the nous and vous forms, e.g. nous allâmes and vous fûtes. Note the circumflex accents.

The other forms are less distinctive and some look like the present tense. However, it should be quite clear from the context whether a text is in the past tense or in the present so you should not mistake verbs in the passé simple for verbs in the present.

To conjugate verbs in the passé simple, verbs can be divided into **four groups**. Here is a table showing the **endings** for each group. To get the stem, you usually remove the ER, IR and RE ending from the infinitive but there are, as always, exceptions.

	GROUP 1	GROUP 2	GROUP 3	GROUP 4
For je	-ai	-is	-us	-ins
For tu	-as	-is	-us	-ins
For il/elle/on	-a	-it	-ut	-int
For nous	-âmes	-îmes	-ûmes	-înmes
For vous	-âtes	-îtes	-ûtes	-întes
For ils/elles	-èrent	-irent	-urent	-inrent

Chapter 8: More Tenses

• The **first group** contains *all* verbs from the ER family, regular and irregular. Remove the –ER ending of the infinitive to get the stem e.g. jouer → jou- (stem).

Examples: je donnai; tu regardas; il alla; nous achetâmes; vous demandâtes; ils bavardèrent.

You may notice that the passé simple endings of the singular forms look like the endings of the future tense. One easy way to differentiate between them is that all endings of the future are preceded by **r**.
Compare: je jouerai = I will play; je jouai = I played

You may also remember that the ER family is the largest family of verbs so there is a strong possibility that an ER verb would be used in any piece of writing featuring the passé simple.

• The **second group** contains all regular IR verbs and all regular RE verbs. It also contains most of the irregular verbs whose past participles end in –it, -i or –is, e.g. dire (past participle = dit); dormir (past participle = dormi); mettre (past participle = mis). And it contains the verbs faire and voir. Remove the IR and RE off the infinitive of regular verbs to get the stem. For some irregular verbs, you need to identify the stem, e.g. dire → stem = d-; dormir → stem = dorm-; mettre → stem = m-; faire → stem = f-; voir → stem = v-.

Examples: je finis; tu vendis; il fit; nous vîmes; vous mîtes; ils dormirent.

• The **third group** contains a group of irregular verbs whose past participles end in –u, e.g. vouloir (past participle = voulu), except voir (second group) and except venir and tenir (fourth group). It also contains the verbs être and mourir. You need to identify the stem for each verb here, e.g. the stem for vouloir is voul-, the stem for être is f- and the stem for mourir is mour-.

Examples: je fus; tu voulus; il mourut; nous vécûmes ; vous courûtes ; ils reçurent.

• And finally, the **fourth group** which contains the two verbs venir and tenir plus all their compound forms such as devenir.
Here are their **passé simple** forms:
Venir: je vins; tu vins; il vint; nous vînmes; vous vîntes; ils vinrent.
Tenir : je tins ; tu tins ; il tint ; nous tînmes ; vous tîntes ; ils tinrent.

Note: When you read a French novel containing dialogue, you can get both the passé simple and the passé composé in the text. The passé simple will be used in the narrative and the passé composé in the speech parts.

Example: Monsieur Duglois **regarda** son reçu et **s'exclama:** "Ah zut ! **J'ai payé** trop cher!"

Complete French Grammar: Part 2

EXERCICES

Identify **all the verbs in the passé simple** in the following extract:

Marie-Claire s'arrêta et regarda autour d'elle. Elle était bien à Mongins mais elle ne reconnaissait plus le village où elle était née. Tout avait changé à ses yeux. Elle alla vers le petit café de la place ; elle entra et commanda une limonade parce qu'elle avait chaud. Les autres clients la regardèrent avec intérêt et lui dirent bonjour. Elle répondit de même et finit sa limonade assez vite. Elle ne voulait pas avoir à expliquer tout de suite ce qu'elle venait faire au village. Tout serait clair jeudi prochain…

LE FUTUR ANTÉRIEUR – FUTURE PERFECT

The last tense we are going to look at in the indicative mood is the **future perfect** or **futur antérieur**.

This is the tense which translates as will have done, e.g. we will have seen three new tenses by the end of this section.

The way you form it in French is very similar to the way it is formed in English. Remember that there is no word will in French. For the future tense, you need to conjugate the verb. Here, you need to put the two auxiliary verbs into the future: avoir and être. To this, you add the past participle of the verb you're using. To go back to the example in the introduction, we will have seen translates as nous aurons vu: we will have = nous aurons + seen = vu.
Avoir in the future: j'aurai; tu auras; il aura; nous aurons; vous aurez; ils auront.
Être in the future: je serai ; tu seras ; il sera ; nous serons ; vous serez ; ils seront.

One important use of the **futur antérieur** is in sentences where one event will have happened before the other. In French, you can write elle me téléphonera quand elle arrivera. Both verbs are in the future, unlike English. It means the two events will coincide: she will phone you *the instant* she arrives. To give the poor girl a bit of time to settle before making the call, the French like to use the future perfect: elle me téléphonera quand elle sera arrivée = she will phone me when (she will have arrived).

EXERCICES

Put the following verbs into the **futur antérieur** and **finish the sentence with a story of your own:**
- Rentrer with on = _____
- Prendre with David = _____
- Visiter with nous = _____
- Finir with les deux sœurs = _____

Chapter 8: More Tenses

We are now going to tackle the **Subjunctive Mood.** We will only deal with **its present tense,** you'll be glad to know!

LE SUBJONCTIF – THE SUBJUNCTIVE

One of the problems with the subjunctive is that it does not really exist in English so there are no foolproof translations to demonstrate when you should use it.

It is used mainly in secondary verb groups, e.g. Je veux (**main verb**, in the present tense) que tu travailles (**secondary verb**, in the subjunctive) sur ta grammaire.

The first thing to realise is that the subjunctive is a common tense in French and that it is hard to avoid using it. In some instances, you *have* to use it.

The way to **conjugate the subjunctive** is not too difficult:

1. For **regular verbs**:
    (a) Find the ils form of the present tense of the verb you want to use and take away the –ent ending to get the stem, e.g. ils voyagent ➝ stem = voyag-
    (b) Add the following endings to the stem:
        For je, add – **e**
        For tu, add – **es**
        For il/elle/ce/ca/on, add – **e**
        For nous, add – **ions**
        For vous, add – **iez**
        For ils/elles, add – **ent**

2. A lot of **irregular verbs** follow the regular verb pattern but as always, there are a few exceptions. Here are the main ones:

Avoir = j'aie; tu aies; il ait; nous ayons; vous ayez; ils aient
Être = je sois; tu sois; il soit; nous soyons; vous soyez; ils soient
Aller = j'aille; tu ailles; il aille; nous allions ; vous alliez ; ils aillent
Faire = je fasse; tu fasses; il fasse; nous fassions; vous fassiez; ils fassent
Prendre = je prenne; tu prennes; il prenne; nous prenions; vous preniez; ils prennent
Venir = je vienne; tu viennes; il vienne; nous venions; vous veniez; ils viennent
Pouvoir = je puisse; tu puisses; il puisse; nous puissions; vous puissiez; ils puissent
Savoir = je sache; tu saches; il sache; nous sachions; vous sachiez; ils sachent
Vouloir = je veuille; tu veuilles; il veuille; nous voulions; vous vouliez; ils veuillent

Complete French Grammar: Part 2

The list below should help you to quickly identify **when to use the subjunctive:**
1. After verbs expressing a wish or a command etc.
2. After verbs expressing emotions such as happiness or fear.
3. After verbs of thinking or believing, used in the negative or in a formal question.
4. After impersonal expressions such as il faut que.
5. After certain conjunctions such as bien que or avant que.
6. After a superlative.

Examples:
1. Je *voudrais* bien que tu viennes au concert avec nous = I'd like you to come to the concert with us/ils *ne veulent pas* que leurs enfants mangent trop de bonbons = They don't want their children to eat too many sweets.
   Note: The subjunctive is used here because the *two subjects are different*. Compare: Elle veut partir = She wants to go where partir is in the infinitive and Elle veut qu'il parte = She wants *him* to go where partir is in the subjunctive.

2. Je *suis contente* que vous soyez là = I'm happy you're here/Il *a peur* qu'elle (ne) tombe = He's afraid she might fall.
   Note: Again, the subjunctive is used because the two subjects are different. Also, when you look at the second sentence, you notice a **ne** in brackets. It is customary to add this **ne** before the verb in the subjunctive after the expression avoir peur que even though the verb is not in the negative. This practice is slowly disappearing in casual speech but not in formal writing.

3. Il *ne croit pas* que ce **soit** vrai = He doesn't believe it's true/Pensez-vous qu'ils **aient** le temps? = Do you think they might have the time?
   Note: Again, the subjunctive is used because the two subjects are different. Something to bear in mind also is that when the verb of thinking or believing is in the positive, you do not use the subjunctive with the second verb. Compare: je *ne crois pas* qu'il **soit** à la maison/je crois qu'il **est** à la maison. And when a question is *not* in the formal style of the example above, you do not use a subjunctive either. Compare: Tu penses qu'il **est** à la maison?/Penses-tu qu'il **soit** à la maison? Quite strange, isn't it ?!

4. Il faut que... = it is necessary that.../il faut que j'**achète** du café = I must buy some coffee/Il *est important que* le gouvernement **crée** de nouveaux emplois = It is important that the government create new jobs/Il *est possible qu'*elle **ait** la grippe = It is possible that she has the flu/Il *se pourrait qu'*il **pleuve** = It could happen that it may rain/Il *vaut mieux que* tu me **téléphones** = It's best if you phone me.
   Note: il faut que + subjunctive is commonly used. Il faut que j'y aille is how you say I must be off; quite a casual expression, yet using a subjunctive...

5. Je passerai *avant que* tu **partes** = I'll call in before you leave/Le professeur fait une démonstration *pour que* (or) *afin que* les élèves **sachent** comment faire = The teacher demonstrates so that the students may know how to proceed/*Bien que* (or) *Quoique* Luc **soit** malade, il est allé au bureau = Although Luke is sick, he has gone to the office/Il ne fera pas d'erreur *pourvu qu'*il **prenne** son temps = He won't make a mistake provided he takes his time/Tu vas tout droit *jusqu'à ce que* tu **arrives** au pont = You go straight on until you arrive at the bridge/On ira au cinéma *à moins que* vous **ne vouliez** rester à la maison = We'll go to the cinema unless you want to stay at home.
   Note: The subjunctive *must* be used after these expressions, no choice!
   Pourvu que can also be used in an exclamation to express something you hope will happen, e.g. Pourvu qu'il fasse beau!
   You can see that you should add a **ne** before the verb in the subjunctive with the expression à moins que even though the verb is not in the negative.

6. C'est l'homme *le plus gentil que* je **connaisse** = He's the kindest man I know/Voici le plat le moins épicé que **nous ayons** = Here is the least spicy dish we have.

Note: All these examples show that the subjunctive is preceded by **que** in most cases.

The **past subjunctive** is not difficult to conjugate and can be useful. Think of the passé composé structure. Just put the auxiliary verb into the subjunctive and keep the past participle as it is in the passé composé. By adding the two together, you have a past subjunctive, e.g. je ne pense pas qu'ils **aient fini** = I don't think they have finished.

EXERCICES

First, decide whether you need to put the verb in brackets into the **subjunctive or not**. Then, put that verb in the **correct tense and person**.

1. Mes parents veulent que je (aller) à l'université à Dublin.
2. Je crois que Magali (avoir) la grippe.
3. Il faut que nous (travailler) dur pour les examens.
4. Bien que Ronan (être) irlandais, il parle très bien français.
5. J'ai peur que la situation (s'empirer). s'empirer = **to get worse**; regular verb

Chapter 9: MORE PRONOUNS

In Part One, we had a look at subject pronouns (je, tu, il etc); object pronouns, both direct (le, la, les etc) and indirect (lui, leur etc); reflexive pronouns (me, te, se etc); stressed/disjunctive pronouns (moi, toi etc); and the qui and que relative pronouns.

Pronouns and the Imperative

Before we examine the other pronouns you need to know, let's look at the weird and wonderful things that happen when you use **object pronouns** and **reflexive pronouns** in the **imperative**. Remember, the imperative is the verb tense you use to give advice or orders, e.g. Écoute!/Écoutons!/Écoutez!

If you need to use an **object pronoun with the imperative**, e.g. give them = donne-leur, the pronouns you need for this are moi (= me/to me, e.g. téléphone-moi); toi (= you/to you) and the rest of the ordinary direct or indirect object pronouns, e.g. mange-les = eat *them*; écris-lui = write *to him/her*.
Note the use of the hyphen between the verb and the pronoun, i.e. donne-leur.

However, if your sentence is in the **negative**, *moi* and *toi* become *me* and *te*, and the pronoun goes *before* the verb, e.g. ne *me* ments pas = don't lie to me; ne *les* mangez pas = don't eat them. The hyphen has also disappeared.

If you use a **reflexive verb in the imperative**, the reflexive pronouns are toi; vous; nous and are placed *after* the verb, e.g. lève-toi, réveillez-vous, dépêchons-nous.
In the **negative**, toi becomes te; vous and nous stay the same but all three reflexive pronouns go *before* the verb, e.g. ne *te* lève pas = don't get up; ne *vous* fâchez pas = don't be angry/annoyed.

EXERCICES

1. Replace the highlighted noun with an **object pronoun** and rewrite the sentence.
(a) Écoute **la prof**. _____
(b) Donnez **ce livre** à Jonathan. _____
(c) Donnez ce livre **à Jonathan**. _____
(d) Ne regardons pas **les photos**. _____

2. Translate into French:
(a) Don't phone him! _____
(b) Get up right now! _____
(c) Let's buy it! (*it* being *une Ferrari*) _____
(d) You two (= vous deux), hurry up! _____

Chapter 9: More Pronouns

Object pronouns and the past tenses

Pronouns also interfere with the **avoir** verbs in the past tenses, i.e. verbs that need the auxiliary **avoir** in the **passé composé** and in the **pluperfect**.
With **être** verbs, you have to make the past participle agree with the subject, e.g. il est sorti/elle est sortie; il était tombé/elle était tombée.
This rule does not apply to verbs whose auxiliary is avoir, e.g. il a pris/elle a pris → no change in pris.

But! Once an object pronoun appears, things change! The past participle must now agree but it must agree with the **object pronoun**, not the subject. Look at this example:
Il a pris **le train** - il a pris **la voiture**
We want to replace the highlighted words with an object pronoun. Le train is replaced by **le** (=it) which becomes **l'** because of the vowel starting the next word. La voiture is replaced by **la** which also becomes **l'**. But see what happens to the previously unchanged past participle:
Il a pris **le train** → il **l'**a pris   -   il a pris **la voiture** → il **l'**a pris**e**.

EXERCICES

Replace the highlighted words with the **correct pronoun**. Then, **rewrite the sentence**, placing the pronoun correctly and making the **past participle agree** if necessary.
1. Elle a vendu **sa maison**. _____
2. On a mangé **le gâteau**. _____
3. Ils ont fini **leurs examens**. _____
4. Tu as vu **Guy et Léa** aujourd'hui? _____

Other pronouns
Y / En

The first two extra pronouns we are going to see are the words **y** and **en**. You already know one expression containing **y**: il y a = there is. **Y** and **en** are mostly used to refer to things and ideas, not to people.
They are usually placed between the subject and the verb, e.g. j'**y** suis allé hier = I went there yesterday/j'**en** suis revenu hier = I came back from there yesterday.

Here is a quick guide to help you know how to use these two pronouns. You will notice that **y** is closely associated with the preposition **à**, and **en** is associated with **de**.

Y	Replaces a *place* preceded by a preposition such as à, sur, dans etc.
	Example: je vais **à** Toulouse → j'**y** vais*/il est **dans** sa chambre → il **y** est
	Replaces an *idea* or *thing* preceded by **à**
	Example: je réponds **à** son texto → j'**y** réponds
*When you use the verb aller in the future, there is a clash of vowels between **y** and the letter **i** starting the verb (e.g. j'irai). This sounds unpleasant so if, for example, you want to say I will go there, you shouldn't say j'y + irai but j'irai là-bas.

59

EN Replaces a *place* preceded by de (=from)
Example: nous venons **de Lyon** → nous **en** venons / elle arrive **de la gare** → elle **en** arrive
Replaces an *idea* or *thing* preceded by de
Example: ils sont contents **de leur résultats** → ils **en** sont contents
Replaces a *thing* preceded by a **partitive article** such as du/de la etc or a *thing* or *person* preceded by an expression of quantity or a number
Example: j'achète **du thé** → j'**en** achète / elle a **deux sœurs** → elle **en** a deux.*

*In this example, note the structure in *elle en a deux*. The word sœurs has been replaced by en, but the number has not been replaced. You keep the number in English as well: she has two sisters → she has **two of them**. Notice how the number/quantity is placed after the verb in French (without the de that may have been present in the original expression, e.g. elle a beaucoup de soeurs → elle en a beaucoup.)

Note: When using the verbs penser à and parler de, the structure will change depending on whether you're thinking about/talking about a **thing/idea** or a **person**. Compare these examples:
Je pense **à** mes vacances, j'**y** pense tout le temps = I'm thinking about my holidays, I think about them all the time. Here you use **y** to replace **à mes vacances.**
Je parle **de** mes vacances, j'**en** parle tout le temps = I'm talking about my holidays, I talk about them all the time. Here you use **en** to replace **de mes vacances**.
But:
Je pense **à** mon ami(e), je pense **à lui/ à elle** tout le temps = I'm thinking about my friend, I think about him/her all the time. Here you use **à** plus the correct **stressed/disjunctive pronoun.**
Je parle **de** mon ami(e), je parle **de lui/ d'elle** tout le temps = I'm talking about my friend, I talk about him/her all the time. Here you use **de** plus the correct **stressed/disjunctive pronoun**.
Other verbs where this rule applies: s'intéresser à = to be interested in; s'occuper de = to take care of; se méfier de = to be wary of.

EXERCICES

Replace the highlighted **words** with **the correct pronoun/expression** from this section.
(a) Nous sommes allés **chez ma tante**. _____
(b) Je fais **du hockey** depuis six ans. _____
(c) Il s'intéresse beaucoup **à Isabelle**. _____
(d) J'invite **quarante personnes**. _____
(e) Ils vont **à Paris** en juin mais Patrick ira **à Paris** en septembre.
_____

Chapter 9: More Pronouns

Before we take a look at other types of pronouns, you need to know where the pronouns you saw so far go in a sentence, especially when there is more than one pronoun in the sentence. Here is a handy grid:

Position of pronouns
You read the grid from left to right.

1	2	3	4	5	6	7	8	9	10
je / j' tu il/elle/on/ça nous vous ils/elles	ne/n'	me/m' te/t' se/s' nous vous se/s'	le/l' la/l' les	lui leur	y	en	verb/ auxiliary	pas (or plus/ jamais etc)	past participle

Examples:
Elle m'y conduit (= she drives me there) → elle(1) m'(3) y(6) conduit(8)
Je ne lui en ai pas parlé (= I didn't talk to him/her about it) → je(1) ne(2) lui(5) en(7) ai(8) pas(9) parlé(10)

Note: When your verbal group contains an **infinitive**, e.g. *je vais jouer*, the pronouns that were numbered 3 to 7 in our grid shift to the **right** with the infinitive at the end of the sentence: **1** is still *je, tu, il* etc, **2** is still *ne/n'* but now we have the verb/auxiliary in **3**, number **4** is *pas* or the other negatives, and **5** is the past participle. We then have the original pronouns in columns 3, 4, 5, 6, 7 as numbers **6, 7, 8, 9** and **10**. Number **11** is the infinitive.

Examples: Elle va m'y conduire (= she is going to drive me there)
Je n'ai pas pu lui en parler (= I was not able to talk to him/her about it)

EXERCICES

Replace the **highlighted words** with the **appropriate pronoun**. Then, **rewrite** the sentence, putting the pronouns in the correct place.
(a) Je n'ai pas vu **Béatrice/au café**.
(b) Il ne faut pas donner **de lait/à mon chat**; il ne tolère pas le lait.
(c) Elle donne **son ticket/au chauffeur de bus**.
(d) Elle donne **deux tickets/au chauffeur de bus**.
(e) Elle donne **ses deux tickets/au chauffeur de bus**.

Complete French Grammar: Part 2

As mentioned already, there are other types of pronouns, such as **possessive pronouns**, **interrogative pronouns** and **demonstrative pronouns**.

Possessive pronouns

These are the words you use when you want to say mine and yours. They need to agree with the noun they replace, even though that noun does not appear.

	Replacing a masculine singular noun:	Replacing a feminine singular noun:	Replacing a masculine plural noun:	Replacing a feminine plural noun:
MINE	le mien	la mienne	les miens	les miennes
YOURS, casual	le tien	la tienne	les tiens	les tiennes
HIS / HERS	le sien	la sienne	les siens	les siennes
OURS	le nôtre	la nôtre	les nôtres	les nôtres
YOURS, polite or group	le vôtre	la vôtre	les vôtres	les vôtres
THEIRS	le leur	la leur	les leurs	les leurs

Example: J'ai trouvé **un sac**. – Oh merci, c'est **le mien!**

Another example is what some French people say when they are toasting each other's health with a drink. Health is santé, a feminine noun. People can say À ta santé! or if more formal, À votre santé! But they can also say À la tienne! or À la vôtre! which implies the word santé.

Note that if you want to say it is mine, yours etc, possessive pronouns can be replaced by **c'est à + stressed pronoun**, e.g. c'est le mien/la mienne → c'est à moi; c'est le leur/la leur → c'est à eux. As you can see, the beauty of this structure is that it does not reflect what's being 'owned'. It reflects only the 'owner', making it easier to use.

You also use this structure to express it's my turn etc and it's up to me etc, e.g. C'est à moi de jouer = it's my turn to play; c'est à elle de s'excuser = it's up to her to apologise.

EXERCICES

Translate the following sentences into French:
(a) My car is black but his is blue.
(b) (addressing a friend) These pens, are they mine or yours?
(c) (addressing Monsieur Calvé) These pens, are they mine or yours?
(d) Your house is big but ours is small.

Chapter 9: More Pronouns

Interrogative pronouns

You all know **question words** like qui (= who) and qu'est-ce que (= what) in questions such as qui habite là? (= who lives there?) and qu'est ce que tu fais? (= what are you doing?). What you might not have known is that you were using **interrogative pronouns**.
Here are a few extra details about these types of words.

Qui can be used **with a preposition**, e.g. Avec qui est-ce que tu vas en ville? = With whom are you going to town?/Who are you going to town with?

In the expression qu'est ce que, the first word is **que**, and that is the actual pronoun what (remember that qu'est-ce que translates as what is it that). In formal style, you can use the word que as the only question word for what but in that case, the verb-subject structure is inverted. Compare: Qu'est-ce que tu fais?/Que fais-tu?
Note: When what is the subject, you need to say qu'est ce **qui**; e.g. qu'est-ce qui est arrivé? = what happened?
When que is used with a preposition, it changes to quoi; e.g. à quoi tu penses? = what are you thinking about?

Quel(s)/quelle(s) (= which) are not interrogative pronouns because even though they can be used to ask questions, they do not replace nouns. However, they are used to phrase the interrogative pronoun which one(s).
Here is how to say which one(s) in French:
Masculine singular: **lequel** (i.e. le + quel, both in the masculine singular)
  Feminine singular: **laquelle**
    Masculine plural: **lesquels**
      Feminine plural: **lesquelles**
Example: J'ai aimé un de ses livres (I liked one of his books) – Ah oui? Lequel? (Oh yes? Which one?)
(Un livre is masculine singular).

EXERCICES

Fill in the gaps with the correct interrogative pronoun:
(a) J'ai vu une de ses sœurs. – Ah oui ? _____?
(b) J'ai pris deux de tes stylos. – Ah bon? _____?
(c) Avec _____ est-ce que tu as payé, avec ta carte bancaire ou par chèque?
(d) Voici mes T-shirts, _____ tu préfères, le blanc ou le rose?
(e) _____ lisez-vous?
(f) Il est pour _____, ce bouquet de fleurs?

Demonstrative pronouns

These are words such as: **the one** or **this one, these ones**.

	Used for the one(s) followed by qui (who) or que (which/that)	Used for this/that one and these/those ones*
Masculine singular	celui	celui-ci / celui-là
Feminine singular	celle	celle-ci / celle-là
Masculine plural	ceux	ceux-ci / ceux-là
Feminine plural	celles	celles-ci / celles-là

*You may remember ci and là from when we discussed **demonstrative adjectives**. They help with the distinction between this/these and that/those.

EXERCICES

Translate the following sentences into French:
(a) Here are some ice creams, take the one you want.
(b) These shoes are horrible but those ones are nice!
(c) Mushrooms? Do you want these ones or those ones?

_____
_____
_____

Other relative pronouns

In Part 1, we studied the relative pronouns qui and que. Their role is to link up parts of sentences, e.g. je parle du garçon **qui** a les cheveux roux et **que** j'ai rencontré le week-end dernier = I'm talking about the boy **who** has red hair and **whom** I met last weekend.

There are other relative pronouns. Although some are identical to interrogative pronouns, their job here is to link up parts of sentences.

- **Où** is used to indicate place or time, e.g. la ville où je suis né = the town where I was born; l'année où je suis né = the year (when) I was born.

- **Dont** is used to express of which/of whom, whose, from which/from whom, when the original expression contains de, e.g. l'auteur de ce livre est irlandais = the author of this book is Irish → voici un livre dont l'auteur est irlandais = here is a book whose author is Irish.

- **Quoi** is used to express with what, on what, etc. It is preceded by a preposition and never refers to people or to specific things, e.g. le sculpteur leur a montré **avec quoi** il travaille = the sculptor showed them **with what** he works/what he works with.

Chapter 9: More Pronouns

- **Ce qui; ce que; ce dont** are used to express what, e.g. je ne sais pas **ce qui** est arrivé = I don't know **what** happened; tu as entendu **ce que** Thomas a dit? = did you hear **what** Thomas said?; dites-moi **ce dont** vous avez besoin = tell me **what** you need.

Note: Ce dont is only used when the original expression contained de, e.g. parler de = to talk of/about; avoir besoin de = to need, etc. Nowadays, **de quoi** is often used to replace the very formal **ce dont**; e.g. je sais de quoi il parle replaces je sais ce dont il parle.

- **Lequel/laquelle/lesquels/lesquelles** are used to express of which/whom, about which/whom and are used when referring to specific things and people.
  As you can see, they all contain a definite article, making things quite specific. They are used with a preposition, e.g. les voisins **avec lesquels** je m'entends le mieux sont les Martin = the neighbours **with whom** I get on best are the Martins.

You need to use this structure when you say the reason why = la raison pour laquelle.

Note: Be careful when the preposition is **à**. À + lequel will become **auquel** and à + lesquels/lesquelles will become auxquels/auxquelles, as was the case for à + le (→ au) and à + les (→ aux).
Example: penser à = to think about → le gâteau auquel je pense est dans le frigo = the cake I'm thinking about is in the fridge.

EXERCICES

Fill in the gaps with a relative pronoun covered in this section. Then, translate your sentence into English.

(a) L'homme _____ la maison a brûlé est portugais.
_____

(b) Le village _____ j'habite est très petit.
_____

(c) La lettre _____ je vais répondre arrivera lundi.
_____

(d) Je ne sais pas _____ je vais mettre pour le baptême.
_____

(e) Le jour _____ on est allés au parc, il faisait très beau.
_____

(f) De _____ est-ce que vous parlez?
_____

Part 3: The Sentence
Troisième Partie: La Phrase
Chapter 10: Putting the Jigsaw Together

You now have enough jigsaw pieces to make a beautiful picture! We will therefore finish with a chapter on the sentence.

You know that not all sentences are the same, e.g. compare this sentence: Arrête! to this one: Toute la famille Duclos s'était retrouvée à l'occasion de l'anniversaire du grand-père Marcel qui fêtait ses quatre-vingts ans.

We are going to have a look at different styles of sentences, and examine where problems may arise.

Direct speech: Discours direct/ Indirect speech: Discours indirect

In a text, you may come across a quote. This is what we call **direct speech**, e.g. Julien dit: 'J'ai faim' (= Julien says: 'I'm hungry').

However, you could also see: Julien dit qu'il a faim (=Julien says that he is hungry). That is **indirect speech**. You're **reporting** what is said instead of **quoting** what is said.

You can see that the structure has changed slightly in the indirect speech. For a start, you've had to change the I subject in the quote to he and change the verb to suit. This is important if you have to answer a question in French in an exam. Have a look at the following example:

Example:
Text: Mon père me dit tout à coup: 'Je me sens vieux, tu sais'.
(= My father told me all of a sudden: 'I feel old, you know')
Question: Que dit le père de l'auteur soudainement?
(= What does the author's father suddenly say?)
Answer: Le père de l'auteur dit qu'il se sent vieux.
(=The author's father says that he feels old.)

The best way to answer the question is to use **indirect speech** to report what was said in the quote. You must however manipulate the quote to adapt it for indirect speech:

You need to add que between the two parts of the sentence and you need to alter the verb since you need to change je to il: **Je me sens** (reflexive verb) → **il se sent**

Also, when you write using indirect speech in French, you may need to change the tense used in the quote, depending on the tense used in the first verb (i.e. the **reporting** verb such as say).

Compare:

Direct speech: Indirect speech:

Julien **dit** 'J'ai faim'   →   Julien **dit** qu'il **a** faim
Julien **a dit** 'J'ai faim' →   Julien **a dit** qu'il **avait** faim

Chapter 10: Putting the Jigsaw Together

This is how it works:
- When the **first verb** is in the **présent**, e.g. Julien dit (= Julien says), or in the **futur**, e.g. Julien dira (= Julien will say), the **second verb** used in the indirect speech stays in the same tense as in the quote.

Examples:
Julien dit (*présent*): 'J'ai (*présent*) faim' (= Julien says: 'I'm hungry') → Julien **dit** (*présent*) qu'**il a** (*présent*) faim (= Julien says that he is hungry)
Julien **dira** (*futur*): 'J'avais (*imparfait*) faim' (= Julien will say: 'I was hungry') → Julien **dira** (*futur*) qu'il **avait** (*imparfait*) faim (= Julien will say that he was hungry)

- When the **first verb** is in the **past**, the **second verb** may not stay in the same tense in the indirect speech as in the quote. Here are the instances when the second verb changes tense:

Julien a **dit** (*passé composé*): 'J'ai faim' (*présent*) → Julien **a dit** qu'il **avait** faim (*imparfait*)
Julien a **dit** (*passé composé*) : 'J'ai eu faim' (*passé composé*) → Julien **a dit** qu'il **avait eu** faim (*plus-que-parfait*)
Julien **a dit** (*passé composé*): 'J'**aurai** faim' (*futur*) → Julien **a dit** qu'il **aurait** faim (*conditionnel présent*)

QUOTE	REPORTED SPEECH
Présent→	Imparfait
Passé Composé→	Plus-Que-Parfait
Futur→	Conditionnel Présent

This rule also applies when the first verb is in the **imparfait**, e.g. Julien disait (= Julien was saying/Julien used to say); in the **passé simple**, e.g. Julien dit (= Julien said); and in the **plus-que-parfait**, e.g. Julien avait dit (= Julien had said).

EXERCICES

Read the text below and answer the questions that follow in French:
« Il va y avoir un orage, c'est sûr. Tu es d'accord pour rentrer? » dit Jean-Baptiste à son ami Erwan. Erwan regarda le ciel et soupira. Il répondit « Je n'ai pas pris un seul poisson! ». Leur partie de pêche se terminait bien trop tôt. Mais Jean-Baptiste avait raison, le ciel était vraiment menaçant. Erwan dit: « Bon, ok, on ramasse tout notre matériel et on y va. Mais j'espère que les filles comprendront pourquoi il n'y aura pas de poisson pour le barbecue de ce soir! »

Questions:
1. Qu'a demandé Jean-Baptiste à Erwan au début du texte?
2. Qu'a répondu Erwan?
3. Qu'a dit Erwan dans la dernière phrase du texte?

Complete French Grammar: Part 3

The Passive Voice: La Voix Passive

The active voice (la voix active) is used more frequently but the passive voice has its uses as well.

The passive voice is when instead of the subject doing an action, the **subject has an action done to it**.

Compare: le jury choisit le vainqueur (active voice) (= the jury chooses the winner) to le vainqueur est choisi par le jury (passive voice) (= the winner is chosen by the jury).

The passive voice was used when we dealt with the uses of the **passé composé** and the **Imparfait** in Part 1. It was le voleur n'a pas été retrouvé (= the robber was not found again).

The **grammatical subject** of any sentence tends to be the centre of attention so that's why, sometimes, the passive voice is used.
Compare these two sentences:
Le club de tennis a organisé un repas = The tennis club organised a dinner. (**active voice**)
Le repas a été organisé par le club de tennis = The meal was organised by the tennis club. (**passive voice**)

It's the fact that it's the *tennis club* doing the organising that is more important in the first sentence, whereas it's *the meal* that is the focus of the second sentence.
So by making the **direct object** of the first sentence (the meal) the subject of the second sentence, the story changes focus.

Note: It's only when you have a **direct** object that you can switch the focus this way. It can't be done with an **indirect** object. This means that very common phrases in English such as I was told cannot happen in French because to tell is dire à, which has to have an indirect object. One way to translate I was told is to use the neutral on (i.e. not in the sense of we) and keep your sentence in the active voice, e.g. on m'a dit…

You may also have to use the **passive voice** when the original subject is unclear or even unknown, e.g. la voiture a été volée = the car was stolen. Stolen by whom? Who knows?

The passive voice can be used in all tenses; there is just a little adjustment to make:
You must identify the **past participle** of the verb you're using. Before that past participle, you will put the verb **être** in the tense required. You do the same in English, e.g. I will help/ **I will be** helped.

Chapter 10: Putting the Jigsaw Together

We'll use the verb aider = to help

TENSE	ACTIVE VOICE	PASSIVE VOICE
PASSÉ COMPOSÉ	il a aidé	il a été aidé
PASSÉ SIMPLE	Il aida	Il fut aidé
PLUS-QUE-PARFAIT	Il avait aidé	Il avait été aidé
IMPARFAIT	il aidait	il était aidé
PRÉSENT	il aide	il est aidé
FUTUR	il aidera	il sera aidé
CONDITIONNEL PRÉSENT	il aiderait	il serait aidé
CONDITIONNEL PASSÉ	Il aurait aidé	Il aurait été aidé
SUBJONCTIF	qu'il aide	qu'il soit aidé

When you look closely at all the passive voice structures here, you notice that aidé, the past participle of aider, is used in all cases. You can also see that the verb être is in the tense named on the left in the TENSE column,
e.g. il sera aidé → il sera = he will be (être in the Future) + aidé = helped (past participle of aider)

Note: Watch out for the possible **agreement of the past participle with the subject**, e.g. il sera aidé but elle sera aidée/ils seront aidés/elles seront aidées, due to the use of the verb être.

For the passive voice in the **passé immédiat** and the **futur proche**, keep the verbs venir de and aller in the present. Use the infinitive être along with the past participle you need, e.g. il vient d'être aidé; il va être aidé (= he is going + to be + helped)

EXERCICES

Switch the focus of the following sentences by putting them into the passive voice:
(a) Le boulanger fait les baguettes.
(b) La police a capturé le voleur.
(c) Les garçons prépareront le repas.
(d) L'agence de voyage organisait les tickets.
(e) Le professeur va aider les élèves.

Complete French Grammar: Part 3

Asking Questions

The three ways of asking questions to which the answer is oui or non are:
1. Using a statement with a question mark , e.g. Tu aimes le tennis?
2. Using est-ce que before the statement, e.g. Est-ce que tu aimes le tennis?
3. Using a verb-subject switch, e.g. Aimes-tu le tennis?

Note: 1 and 2 are quite casual questions, whereas 3 is quite formal.

You may also need to use **question words and expressions**:
- how = comment
- how much/many = combien
- how long = combien de temps
- what = qu'est-ce que/que
- when = quand
- where = où
- in what place = à quel endroit/en quel lieu
- which (sometimes translated as 'what' in English) = quel(s)/quelle(s)
- which one(s) = lequel/laquelle/lesquels/lesquelles
- who = qui
- why = pourquoi
- for what reason = pour quelle raison

The usual **position of question words** is right at the beginning of a sentence but this is not a necessity, e.g. Combien de temps as-tu passé en Vendée? is the same as Tu as passé combien de temps en Vendée? (= how long did you spend in the Vendée region?).

In formal questions containing a verb-subject switch, you may see some structures that can be puzzling.

In French, you can't ask why is the author sad? using a word for word translation. You have to say why + the author + is + he + sad? = pourquoi l'auteur est-il triste? This is because there is a **noun** in the formal question. Without the noun present, you can translate why is he sad? word for word = pourquoi est-il triste?

On that point, if you have to **answer** this type of question, be sure not to put in that second subject in your answer. The correct way to answer our question Pourquoi l'auteur est-il triste? is: l'auteur est triste parce que…, **not** l'auteur est-il triste parce que…. The il has to be taken out.

EXERCICES

Translate each of the following questions into French twice, once in a casual style, then in a formal manner.
(a) How long did you stay in Spain? (Remember: to stay = rester)
(b) Why are the shops closed?
(c) What car will they buy?

_____

_____

_____

The Negative Sentence: La Phrase Négative

You sometimes need to put a sentence into the negative to express what you **don't do**, what you **don't do anymore**, what you **never** do, etc.
Here are the most common negative expressions:
   not = ne … pas
   not anymore = ne … plus
   never = ne … jamais
   nobody = ne … personne
   nothing = ne … rien
   only = ne … que
(**Note:** If you want to say *only … left*, you use **ne … plus que**,
e.g. je **n'**ai **plus que** deux euros = I've only got two euro left.)

Remember that the verb goes between the ne and the other part of the negative (e.g. pas) if your verb consists of one word, e.g. je *regarde* → je **ne** *regarde* **pas**.

If you're using a verb construction of more than one word, like when you use the **passé composé** or the **futur immédiat**, ne and pas/plus/jamais/rien frame the **first part** of the verb construction, e.g. il a mangé → il **n'a pas** mangé/on va s'amuser → on **ne** va **pas** s'amuser. However, when you use ne… personne or ne… que, you must put personne and que after the verbal group, e.g. il **n'**a vu **personne**/il **ne** va voir **personne**/nous **n'**avons vu **que** ce film/nous **n'**allons voir **que** ce film.
Incidentally, if you want to start a sentence with nobody, use personne first, then add the ne, e.g. nobody went to the party = **personne n'**est allé à la fête.

If a sentence contains **object pronouns**, such pronouns stay close to one-word verbs in the negative, e.g. je le vois (= I see him/it) → je ne le vois pas (I don't see him/it). If your verb contains more than one word, keep the pronoun close to the first verb in the negative, e.g. je l'ai vu → je ne l'ai pas vu, except in the case of a verb + infinitive structure, e.g. je vais le voir → je ne vais pas le voir. (See the section on Pronouns)

Complete French Grammar: Part 3

EXERCICES

Put the following sentences into the negative, using a suitable negative expression. Then **translate** what you wrote into English:
(a) Philippe aime le foot, il va regarder le match de foot à la télé ce soir.
(b) J'ai vu le film *Autant En Emporte Le Vent* (= *Gone With The Wind*)
(c) Il me reste quatre bonbons.
(d) Vous lui avez téléphoné?

_____
_____
_____
_____

Common Problems in Sentence Writing

We are now going to look at some problems and how to solve them!

1. Connaître vs Savoir

Connaître and savoir are the two verbs used in French to express *to know*. Here is a foolproof way of knowing which one to use; the trick is to use *grammar!*
Quite simply, use connaître with nouns and savoir with anything else.

Examples:

Je connais … la route/ cet homme/ deux de ses livres/ sa mère/ l'Italie etc…
Je sais … nager/ ce qu'il faut faire/ tout/ que j'ai raison etc…

EXERCICES

Translate the following sentences into French:
(a) He knows my sister's friend.
(b) We know how to speak French.
(c) I know that it's difficult.
(d) Do you know this film?

_____
_____
_____
_____

Chapter 10: Putting the Jigsaw Together

2. Anybody and everybody!

If you have ever found it hard to remember the French for expressions such as everything, nothing or something, have a look at the following lists. They might help!

Somebody/someone = **quelqu'un**
e.g. il y a quelqu'un à la porte = there's someone at the door
Somebody else = **quelqu'un d'autre**
e.g. je téléphonerai à quelqu'un d'autre = I'll phone somebody else
Anybody = **n'importe qui**
e.g. n'importe qui peut s'inscrire = anybody can join
Each one = **chacun/chacune**
e.g. chacun ses goûts! = each to his or her own!   (Note: each = chaque)
A few people = **quelques personnes**
e.g. j'ai vu quelques personnes = I saw a few people
Some people say = **certains disent que/il y en a qui disent que**
People say = on dit que
e.g. on dit qu'il faut faire attention ici = some people say you have to be careful here
Nobody = **personne**
e.g. On sonne, j'ouvre, personne! = the doorbell rings, I open the door, nobody there!
Everybody = **tout le monde**
e.g. tout le monde était là = everybody was there

Something = **quelque chose**
e.g. je vais te dire quelque chose = I'm going to tell you something
Something else = **quelque chose d'autre/autre chose**
e.g. il vous faut autre chose? = do you need anything else?
Anything = **n'importe quoi**
e.g. il ferait n'importe quoi pour elle = he'd do anything for her
(**Note:** N'importe quoi can be used to express nonsense/rubbish
e.g. il dit n'importe quoi =he talks nonsense)
Nothing = **rien**
e.g. rien n'a changé = nothing has changed/ne … rien
e.g. je n'ai rien fait = I did nothing/I didn't do anything
Everything = **tout**
e.g. tout doit disparaitre = everything must go

Some (people or things) = **certains/certaines**
e.g. certains ont voyagé en train = some travelled by train
No + noun = **aucun(e)(s)**
e.g. il n'a aucun tact = he has no tact
Not one (person or things) = **aucun/aucune**
e.g. aucun n'a réagi = not one (person) reacted

73

Somewhere = **quelque part**
e.g. je l'ai déjà vu quelque part = I've seen him somewhere before
Somewhere else/elsewhere = **autre part/ailleurs**
e.g. j'irai ailleurs l'année prochaine = I'll go elsewhere next year
Anywhere = **n'importe où**
e.g. garez-vous n'importe où = park anywhere
Nowhere = **(ne …) nulle part**
e.g. on n'est allés nulle part = we went nowhere/we didn't go anywhere
Everywhere = **partout**
e.g. il y avait de l'eau partout = there was water everywhere

Sometimes = **quelquefois / parfois**
e.g. quelquefois, j'achète du caviar = sometimes, I buy some caviar
From time to time = **de temps en temps**
e.g. on court de temps en temps = we run from time to time
Sometime/someday = **un jour**
e.g. j'irai à Bali un jour = I'll go to Bali someday
Once, twice, etc… = **une fois, deux fois etc…**
e.g. il était une fois… = once upon a time…
Another time = **une autre fois**
e.g. on ira au parc une autre fois = we'll go to the park another time
Anytime = **n'importe quand / à n'importe quelle heure**
e.g. vous pouvez venir à n'importe quelle heure = you can call in anytime
Never = **(ne …) jamais**
e.g. elle ne boit jamais = she never drinks
Each time = **chaque fois**/**Every time** = **à chaque fois**
e.g. je perds à chaque fois = I lose every time
Each day = **chaque jour**/**Everyday** = **tous les jours**
e.g. on va là tous les jours = we go there every day
All the time = **tout le temps**
e.g. il sourit tout le temps = he smiles all the time
Always = **toujours**
e.g. il a toujours faim = he's always hungry

(**Note:** Toujours can be used to express still, e.g. tu as toujours ta vieille voiture? = do you still have your old car? Encore can be used in the same way, e.g. tu as encore faim? = are you still hungry?)

Grammar Terms in French

adjective (e.g. big, green, etc.) = adjectif qualificatif
adverb = adverbe
article = article or déterminant
auxiliary = auxilliaire
conditional = conditionnel
conjunction = conjonction
definitite article = article défini
demonstrative adjective = adjectif démonstratif
demonstrative pronoun = pronom démonstratif
direct object = objet direct
feminine = féminin
future = futur
immediate future = futur immédiat or futur proche
immediate past = passé immédiat
imperative = impératif
imperfect = imparfait
indefinite article = article indéfini
indicative mood = mode indicatif
indirect object = objet indirect
infinitive = infinitif
interrogative pronoun = pronom interrogatif
irregular = irrégulier

masculine = masculin
mood = mode
noun = nom
partitive article = article partitif
past = passé
past historic = passé simple
past participle = participe passé
perfect tense = passé composé
pluperfect = plus-que-parfait
plural = pluriel
possessive adjective = adjectif possessif
possessive pronoun = pronom possessif
preposition = préposition
present = présent
present participle = participe présent
present tense = présent (de l'indicatif)
pronoun = pronom
reflexive pronoun = pronom réfléchi
reflexive verb = verbe pronominal
regular = régulier
relative pronoun = pronom relatif
singular = singulier
stressed / disjunctive pronoun = pronom forme forte
subject = sujet
subjunctive = subjonctif
tenses = temps
verb = verbe

Complete French Grammar: Part 3

EXERCICES

Read the text and then **pick out the 20 grammar elements** listed below.

Mon chien s'appelle Nestor. Croyez-moi, c'est mon chien à moi, c'est le mien. C'est moi qui le promène et qui lui donne à manger. Il dort dans ma chambre sur mon lit. Quelquefois, il faut que je le pousse, il prend tellement de place, mais je ne dormirais pas bien s'il n'était pas là.

L'autre jour, on est allés se promener dans le parc, Nestor et moi. Il faisait un temps magnifique. Soudain, un homme qui s'était approché furtivement, a pris mon sac et s'est enfui en courant. Nestor est parti à sa poursuite et a réussi à l'arrêter! J'ai récupéré mon sac, le voleur a dû aller au commissariat et Nestor, lui, a eu droit à un énorme bisou! Ce soir-là, il a pris toute la place sur le lit mais je ne l'ai pas poussé…

Trouvez dans le texte un exemple de:

1. Un adjectif possessif
2. Un pronom possessif
3. Un pronom personnel sujet
4. Un pronom objet direct
5. Un pronom objet indirect
6. Un pronom forme forte
7. Un verbe à l'infinitif
8. Un verbe au présent de l'indicatif
9. Un verbe au passé composé
10. Un verbe à l'imparfait
11. Un verbe au plus-que-parfait
12. Un verbe au subjonctif
13. Un verbe à l'impératif
14. Un verbe au conditionnel présent
15. Un adverbe
16. Un participe présent
17. Un adjectif démonstratif
18. Un adjectif qualificatif au masculin singulier
19. Un pronom relatif
20. Un verbe pronominal à l'infinitif

Bon courage pour votre travail!